FORGIVENESS
UNFORGETTABLE

Nikki Lee Brannon

WWW.NIKKILEE_BRANNON@YAHOO.COM
PHOTO CREDITS: TIPLYASHINA EVGENIYA
BOOK AND COVER DESIGN BY: NIKKI LEE BRANNON/FIVERR
NLB PUBLISHING

ISBN: 9780692478912
FIRST EDITION: MAY 2015

ISBN: 0692478914

DEDICATION

I LOVINGLY DEDICATE THIS STORY OF SURVIVAL AND FORGIVENESS TO EACH OF MY SIBLINGS AND MY PRECIOUS MAMA WHO SHARED THIS LIFE WITH ME. I THANK GOD FOR THE MERCY HE SHOWED MY DADDY IN HIS LAST DAYS ON EARTH. I PRAY OUR STORY CAN BE USED TO SOFTEN THE MOST HARDENED HEART THAT BLAMES GOD FOR THE SUFFERINGS THEY HAVE FACED. IF HE CAN FORGIVE US FOR ALL THAT WE'VE DONE WRONG, WHO ARE WE NOT TO FORGIVE EVEN OUR WORST ENEMY AND SOMETIMES OUR WORST ENEMY IS MANIFESTED IN OUR VERY OWN FAMILY.

AKNOWLEDGEMENTS

*...T*O MY LOVING, SUPPORTIVE HUSBAND, WHO NEVER STOPPED BELIEVING I COULD SHARE THIS AND BE HEALED OF THE PAST. I LOVE YOU AND I AM SO THANKFUL FOR YOUR UNDYING SUPPORT FOR ALL GOD HAS LED ME TO DO IN THIS LIFE AND I AM ETERNALLY GRATEFUL THAT I GOT TO SHARE IT WITH YOU!*

...TO MY DEAR COUSIN, RAE LYNN, WHO SPENT COUNTLESS HOURS IN FAITHFUL SUPPORT HELPING ME THROUGH THE EDITING PROCESS, I LOVE AND APPRECIATE YOUR WILLING HEART TO ASSIST ME IN THE COMPLETION OF MY STORY.

TABLE OF CONTENTS

INTRODUCTION

*"Come and hear, all that fear God, and I will declare
what He hath done for my soul." (Psalm 66:16 KJV)*

Forgiveness is such a powerful thing. It forces us to face the past head-on and conquer it or surrender to it. It makes no excuses, reveals ALL secrets, and offers a refuge of healing and strength to a wounded soul.

Part of my past that I thought I had conquered, and buried forever came back to slap me right in the face. I suddenly realized that I had not released the past, and I had not been honest with myself about this situation at all. I had simply pushed it so far down into the darkest corners of my soul so that I wouldn't have to see it or hear it again. Jesus knew it was still there, but I never prayed about it or spoke to this person about it or confronted the person who had hurt me the most—my father. I thought I could just ignore it for the rest of my life. Packing it away became my coping mechanism. The old cliché, "What doesn't kill us, makes us stronger," was my motto. Jesus knew just how much holding this in was killing me.

I will start by telling you that I know what it's like to live in turmoil, to be impoverished, in constant fear, anxiety, and to be one of many victims of domestic violence due to alcoholism. I also know that the only way I survived is through the mercy of Jesus Christ! My Mama was a Godly woman who was somehow able to get the message of salvation across to me in the midst of impossible circumstances.

I love my parents. This is in no way meant to embarrass or disrespect my family. My father finally got clean and sober the last 15 years of his life. I am very proud of him for that. For the last 6 months of his life, I had those old feelings creeping back up to the surface, and God had to deal with me on showing the forgiveness of Christ. If Jesus could forgive ME, a person who did not deserve his love and forgiveness, how could I possibly call myself a Christian if I had not truly forgiven the one who had hurt me? I did not realize that I still held unforgiveness in my heart.

I thank God for the trials that brought that reality to my attention. *"Beloved, think it not strange concerning the fiery trial which is to try you, as though some strange thing happened to you: But rejoice, inasmuch as ye are partakers of Christ's sufferings; that, when his glory shall be revealed, ye may be glad also with exceeding joy!" (1 Peter 4:12-13 KJV)*

Oh, but it is so hard when we are going through our fiery trials to ever think about it being a blessing! We moan and groan and complain like we're the only ones who has ever faced anything on the planet! *"For I reckon that the sufferings of this present time are NOT WORTHY to be compared with the GLORY which shall be revealed in us." (Romans 8:18 KJV)*

I have been through many fiery trials in my life. I have not been through them alone! Even when I turned my back on God, He still kept me because He knew what He called me to do, and He knew I would someday find my way back.

CHAPTER 1
IN THE SHADOW OF THY WINGS

I WAS RAISED IN A RURAL, FARM TOWN IN SOUTH ALABAMA by Marie, a strong, faithful, Christian woman, and a muscular, hard-working man named Colby. Mama was so gentle and kind, and Daddy was so extremely violent and mean due to his constant intake of alcohol on a daily basis.

I was number seven out of eight children born to my parents. They were in order: Colby Jr., Dan, Ray, (who only lived 12 hours), Ron, Vern, Stephen, Nikki (me), and baby sister, Carol.

Daddy had been married for two years before he married Mama and had a daughter named Dana. I use to sit and daydream about Dana, hoping to meet her someday. I yearned to know her and have her be a part of my life. As a small child, I already understood why it would not be a good idea if Dana were around us. We didn't even want any of our very few friends at school to come home with us because we were too poor, and we were much too scared to leave to spend the night away from home. I remember thinking that, if I left home, I would be constantly worried what would happen to my brothers, sister, and Mama. The days and nights were filled with terror, but the nights were always worse.

Sometimes, Daddy would stay gone all day long and we would get a little reprieve. By nightfall, just when we thought he wasn't coming home, up the driveway he came, car motor racing and revving up like a hotrod about to begin a race, "drunk as a skunk." (southern slang for extremely drunk). I remember my little heart about to pound out of my chest each time I heard that sound and I would observe Mama, frightened like a mother hen, gathering her baby chicks under her wing.

I recall one night he came home, and we scrambled. "Now, don't get in his way, y'all," Mama said. "Why don't y'all just run go get into bed and act like you're already asleep?" Mama whispered.

"Yes, ma'am," we replied. "But Mama, we don't want him to hurt you," we cried.

Mama said, "Just say a prayer for me."

Daddy expected Mama to have supper hot, ready, and on the table in front of him no matter what time he decided to come through that door. If she didn't, it was her bad fortune. "Marie, this food is ice cold and not fit for hogs to eat!" Daddy said, as he picked the heavy porcelain plate up and threw it right at her face. Mama ducked down, and the plate crashed against the wall into what seemed like a million pieces.

I watched, begging, pleading, and crying uncontrollably for my Daddy to stop hitting her. "Daddy, please stop!" I screamed.

"She hasn't done anything wrong, Daddy, so please stop hurting my Mama!" Those cries fell on deaf ears as he continued to beat her unmercifully.

Mama was a very strong woman, as well, and that night she was able to get out from under him and get away. He became so enraged that she broke free that he pulled out his gun and began to shoot at her. Mama gathered us all up, and we hid under the front porch near the chimney. It was at that moment as bullets were flying all around us, and my little body was trembling that I felt the presence of Angels for the first time. My fear somehow subsided, and I began to smile and even giggle a little watching him go "round" and "round" the house shooting in the dark, cursing to the top of his lungs, and finally pass out and fall flat on his face in the yard.

"What a relief!" Vern exclaimed.

"Finally some peace and quiet," Ron chimed in.

"Mama," I said, "I love you and I prayed for you like you asked me."

"Thank you so much, baby," Mama said.

She slowly crept out from under the porch and made certain Daddy was still asleep in the dirt and removed the gun from his hand. I looked at my Daddy with unbelievable compassion. How could I feel anything but hate for him? He's so mean and terrible to us. Why do I still care about him lying there in the dirt passed out drunk; I must be crazy.

"Now, y'all can come out, children!" Mama yelled. I ran inside and took an old blanket out of the closet and threw it across Daddy, so he wouldn't be cold. Mama saw me and gave me a half-hearted grin. "Let's go in and try to get some sleep if we can; y'all have school tomorrow," she said.

School? How in the world am I going to be able to concentrate in school tomorrow? I couldn't go anywhere without worrying about Mama. How could he be so mean to her? She was the most precious person I had ever known. She was a Christian, a wonderful Mama, and she tried her very best to keep us from getting hurt. She loved us so much and she believed Daddy would be saved someday. She taught us to pray for him to quit drinking. She believed he had good qualities that were deeply instilled in him by his godly mother and grandmother. He also had a mean streak a mile wide instilled in him by his extremely abusive father. The cycle would definitely end with me and my siblings. We have to accept responsibility for our own actions. No matter how I grew up, I knew I would not allow my family to ever go through what I had witnessed.

I could not wrap my head around the emotions I felt for him. I loved him, I hated him; he was my terror, my nightmares, yet I covered him up as he lay on the ground just as if I thought he was the most wonderful man in the world. I felt so guilty for doing that, yet I still wanted to do it because I was worried about him, too. How could I be? Mama tried to explain that it was because that's who God made me to be.

As I finally climbed into bed, I wrestled with those emotions, tossing and turning, and I thought I should have kicked him in the head; why did I take him a blanket? The Holy Spirit quickened me, and I felt the same real peace settle over me just as I did hiding under the porch behind the chimney. The "Comforter" was on the job.

We only had a few days left, and school would be out for the summer. As all the other kids were planning summer vacations on some fantastic trip with their families, we were planning to get ready to work in the fields with the local farmers, so we could have what we needed to start the next school term. We knew what hard work was from the time we were big enough to talk.

Daddy did construction work much of our childhood, and he would use us on all of his roofing jobs. Roofing is one job I pray I will never have to do again. The scorching heat, the dead of winter, the crispness of fall, or the newness of spring, is never a good time to roof a house! Most of the jobs we got were tearing off the old roof or roofs prior to replacing the new shingles. We never got a new house job. Tearing off an old batch of shingles is the worst part of the roofing experience. Shovel in hand, we would climb a ladder up to the very top of thc house and begin the tedious process of lifting the old shingles up by the head of the nail, digging them out from the wooden roof one-by-one, and sliding them down to the bed of a truck below. I got pretty good at "ringing the bed," as I called it. I knew if I didn't aim just right, I would have to clean up all the mess out of the client's yard, and that would embarrass Daddy so bad. I didn't want to make him mad, and I knew that for a fact.

I remember Daddy got a job roofing Betsy Freeman's house. Betsy was a little rich kid I went to school with. She always wore the prettiest clothes, had the prettiest hairstyles, and sat with the most popular kids in class. Daddy loaded all of us up after school that afternoon to go do this job. "If we work hard and fast, we can get this thing torn off and re-felted before the sun goes down," Daddy stated.

Every one of us kids had a shovel, and we climbed up the ladder to start the job. I had no idea it was Betsy's house until I was totally covered in black, shingle beads that had stuck to the sweat on my skin, my hair was matted to the top of my head, and my clothes were covered in tar. I looked horrible! My hands were covered in blood and dirt as they busted open from the repetitive use of the shovel.

Betsy walked out into her yard that day and began to twirl her baton. As she threw the baton up into the air, it landed right on top of the roof where I was standing. I retrieved the baton and as I looked down on the ground to throw it back to its rightful owner, I suddenly realized it was Betsy. Our eyes met and she was stunned to see me, one of the so-called "trashiest" kids in school look even more "trashy". She burst into laughter as I threw the baton down to her, and she ran into her house to get on the phone to let all of little friends know who her "servant" was.

I was humiliated, and Daddy just kept cussing at me to work faster before the sun went down. Mama always taught me there was a huge difference between being "trashy" and being poor. We were just plain poor, and there was nothing we could do about it at the time, but other folks didn't seem to see it the way Mama did.

Breaktime came and to add insult to injury, Daddy sent me and Carol to the store to buy drinks and sandwiches for all of us. We cried and begged Daddy to let the boys go instead of us. We didn't want anyone else to see us looking like this.

Vern humbly asked, "Can I go for them, Daddy?"

Daddy just yelled, "H---- no!" Shut up all that crying and get your little a--- off this roof and do what I told you, now!" He screamed. I told you to keep your lazy a—up here with me and lay these d--- shingles, Vern, and don't give me no more lip!" Daddy yelled.

We had to climb down off the roof, filthy and crying as we were and walk down the street to the store. Carol and I hid behind every tree we could find on our way to the store each time we heard a car passing.

Standing in line of the store, there were even more kids we went to school with waiting to check out with their parents as we smelled of sweat, tar, and dirt. They pointed, laughed and stared, as we walked out into the street headed back to work. It sure would be hard to face everybody tomorrow in school. I hoped nobody would even mention it. I prayed they would just forget about it, but they didn't.

I was sorely embarrassed, humiliated, and my self-confidence was zero, yet I had an undying sense of self-worth that kept whispering to me over and over again. "You are a child of the King." Mama had raised me in the Word and deeply instilled in my heart, it gently reminded me I was worth more in the eyes of God than any fancy thing on earth.

CHAPTER 2

SURVIVING THE NIGHT

JUST AS I BEGAN TO DRIFT OFF TO SLEEP, it would always happen- my other real-life nightmare would surface. Mama came in bright and early each morning to wake me to get ready for school. Waking up for school every morning was especially hard on me emotionally because of the nightmares I experienced each night. I would re-live the terror that had gone on the night before in my sleep. When Mama would shake me to wake me up, I would instantly start fighting her, swinging and hitting her, telling her "No!" It was not because I was a bad kid and didn't want to go to school that I fought her, but it was because I was in survival mode even in my sleep.

I had to keep an extra secret in the household of dysfunction. Nobody knew but me and Colby, Jr., my eldest brother. When things would finally calm down each night and everybody had gone to sleep, I would be in the middle of another awful, uncontrollable event, awaken from a not so "sound" sleep to a shadowy figure standing over my bed. When I would finally get my eyes open, I would immediately begin to realize that I was being touched inappropriately by my brother.

Quietly screaming at him, "What are you doing?" so as to not wake up the "sleeping bear" passed out in the yard, (Daddy), I would fight Colby, Jr. off with incredible strength for a 7- year-old child. He would quickly leave the room, and I would be in such shock I could never go back to sleep. I'm not sure what age this all started, but my very first memory of this was age 7 after we were all under the porch hiding from Daddy. I could not believe what was happening to me. My 14 -year-old brother was making my life a living hell. It would be years before I would learn that Junior was my half-brother. It never would make it any easier to deal with, though. I was dazed, confused, and sick to my stomach!

After all that we had to endure each night with Daddy...now this? I could not understand how he could do this to me? I was an innocent, young girl who loved Jesus, and I never should have been exposed to sex in this way at such an early age by a sibling at that. I hated him for this.

My thoughts then began to wander to Daddy and how he is supposed to be my protector. I thought, "If I just scream out when Junior comes in the room, Daddy would come save me." Ha! That's a joke. Daddy would blow my brother away with that gun, Mama would then be so hurt, my other siblings would hate both Daddy and Colby, Jr., and I would be the reason for it. I must not tell anyone about this at all. After all, he is still my brother. Yuck! How could I even call him a brother after he has exposed me to this filth? I prayed to God that the first night was the one and only time he'd try anything like that, but it wasn't.

The nightly visits got more and more frequent, as he would sneak into my room multiple times throughout the night, and attempt to get on top of me. I say attempt because my God made me

9

super strong as a child, and I was able to prevent myself from being raped each and every time. He may have got his hands on me every night before I woke up, but he was never able to do what he so wickedly desired to do. Praise God!

When he would climb up on me, I would take my two little feet and press them against his chest, kick him with both feet using my leg muscles, and his body would go flying off me. Lord, how anybody else was able to sleep through all that commotion was a miracle within itself. I was fighting for my innocence each night, and I won!

None of my other brothers ever touched me inappropriately. I could not fathom the reason why Colby, Jr. did. He made me sick! I could not stand him, yet I still had compassion for him enough to carry this extra burden on my own shoulders and not bring the household down any lower than it already was. At seven years of age, I was making adult decisions that I should have never had to make because of the circumstances. I so wanted to get him in trouble, but the kind of trouble I wanted for him would have been death in our house, and I knew that, so I prayed for strength each night.

Some nights I would lie awake all night just waiting for him. I thought, "If I could just be awake when he came in, I could put a stop to it without him touching me." I hated to fall asleep and wake up to the darkness hovering over me. To this day, I sleep with my bedroom door locked up tight. I fought with him most every night. He was so persistent and would not even come around me during the day.

Each morning, Mama would keep her distance as she went in to wake me up and have to block the punches I'd throw at her. I remember feeling so terrible that I lashed out at her, and I would call her over to me and hug her saying, "Mama, sweet Mama; I'm so sorry I hit you." There is no way I was going to tell her why I reacted that way each morning.

CHAPTER 3

UP IN SMOKE

I GOT VERY MINIMAL SLEEP AT NIGHT and yet, I was in the gifted class at school. Having five siblings ahead of me in school gave me an advantage over some of the students there. I learned a lot of school work from my older brothers. I was not able to go to kindergarten because, during that time, parents had to pay a fee to send their kids. We could not afford basic necessities like food, shelter, and clothing, so kindergarten was definitely out of the question for me. So, I started first grade "ahead of the game." At age seven, I was wise beyond my years. I had mastered the art of "suck it up and keep on going." I had also become very close to the Lord, and I knew He was the only reason I was still alive and still "innocent."

Mama was such a great teacher of God's Word. She taught me so much by living an example of the way Jesus expects us to love, but she was growing increasingly concerned for the safety of her children in our home. As we grew older and stronger, we began to fight Daddy off of Mama trying so desperately to shield her from his continued abuse. We grew so tired of seeing her black eyes, busted lips, and bruises around her neck from being strangled nearly to death. We would discuss our frustrations with one another each day and carefully plot what we would do when he arrived home.

Like a well organized military group, we all had "stations" we were to "man" and when trouble started as it always did, we knew what to do. When we heard the roar of the engine of that 1965 Ford Galaxy 500, the lights would go off. Plan "A" was for everybody to pretend to be asleep, including Mama. Avoid it if at all possible, right? Wrong! Plan "B" was to wait and watch for the first punch to be thrown and then attack with all that is in us all at once. We had a small hole in the closet that we used as a look-out. We placed little sister, Carol there. The rest of us were poised, ready for war with our ears placed against the wall, listening for the inevitable beatings as they began in the next room.

One night that would result in a major change in our lives, we heard Carol scream, "He's got her, y'all!" The battle began as we saw Daddy dragging Mama into the kitchen by the hair of her head. An army of little children, ranging in age from 14 all the way down to age 4, rushed in and attacked.

"Vern, you get his knees," said Dan. "Stephen, you get his feet," he said. "Me and Colby, Jr. will get his arms," he screamed. Dan began to shout orders for me, too. "Nikki, you get him in the stomach!" he shouted. Ron climbed on Daddy's back before Dan could yell anything else, and we had him down on the floor in just a few seconds.

He was so shocked and angry we had jumped on him that he began to reach for his pistol he carried in a holster on his hip. Junior began to wrestle with him over the gun, as he slipped it out to use it on us, and thankfully was able to get it away from him.

"Get off of me, you no good young'uns!" Daddy screamed! "What in the ---- do y'all think you're gonna do?" he asked. "Y'all got to turn loose in a second and when you do, you d--- sure better run because I'm gonna kill every one of you little bas-----!" he warned.

At least we got his attention off of Mama. Daddy just laughed as he began to throw all of us, one by one, against the wall, as he staggered to his feet. Mama lay bruised and bleeding in the corner trying so desperately to get up and check on each of us. Daddy stumbled down the steps and out to his car, cussin' us for everything in the book! "I'm gonna kill every last one of y'all when I get home!"

He cranked up the ole car and sped out of the driveway running over the mailbox, cussin', and shooting his pistol up into the air out the driver's side window. POW! POW! POW! The sound of gunfire was familiar around our place, but it always made me tremble. I heard the sound of squealing tires. I walked to the front porch, nervously shaken, and smelled the burning rubber on the blacktop road. I was so glad he was gone for the night, or at least I hoped he was.

My attention turned towards Mama and her concern for each of us. "How is everybody?" she asked. "Is anybody hurt real badly?" Mama asked.

"No ma'am," said Dan. "We are all doing ok, Mama, how are you?" Dan asked.

Mama's face was beginning to swell, and she ran to the bathroom to get a cold, wet washcloth. My heart was still beating 1000 times per minute it seemed, as I heard the sound of that old Galaxy come crashing into the fence.

"Mama, let's go, he's back!" said Vern. Mama could barely walk from the bruises he'd just left her, but she pushed all of us out the back door, and we began to run into the woods to hide. I heard the sound of the car door shut as we took off running. Dan made little Carol climb up on his back, and he carried her. Stephen held my hand, and we ran for our lives.

"Marie! Marie! Where in the h--- are y'all?" he screamed. "I will kill every one of y'all when I find you," he said.

His voiced rang in my ears as it echoed through the trees. I looked back, and I could see him running around the house looking for us. "Don't be hiding from me, young'uns," he yelled. "Y'all got a whooping coming that y'all ain't never gonna forget for trying to jump on your ole Daddy tonight!" He screamed. "Are y'all inside?" he yelled. "I hope y'all are because I'm gonna burn this son of a b---- down with all y'all in it!" he exclaimed. I thought my heart was going to jump right out of my chest.

Deep in the South Alabama woods, we were tired and so weary from the chase. The mosquitoes began to make a feast on our skin, as we sat on the ground leaned up against the tall pine trees listening for the sound of that car to crank back up. Suddenly, the sky lit up the dark night, and there was an orange glow near the house.

"Oh, Mama!" I said. "He's burning down the house!" I cried. We watched in disbelief, as the old rental home we lived in burned to the ground in minutes.

Daddy cranked up the car and drove away. My little brain was so confused. How could he set our house on fire with us in it? He thought we were inside hiding, and he lit a fire to consume us. He didn't know we were in the woods. He was intent on killing us that night in his drunken rage.

We were already so poor. We had nothing and nothing minus nothing is less than nothing! We all began to cry and wonder where we would go and what on earth would we do. Mama softly and calmly began to pray. "Lord, you know the situation we are in, and I need you to give us a safe place to lay our heads tonight," she prayed.

The fire trucks finally made it out to the burning house, and we listened through the woods as they worked tirelessly to extinguish the blaze. The firemen contacted our landlord, Mr. Davis, to let him know his rental house was on fire. Everybody knew everybody in this small town.

Mr. Davis arrived at the property with a look of dread on his face and asked, "Were y'all able to get all of them out?" I rent this little ole house out to Colby and Marie Winslow and their 7 children," he said. "Where are they?" he asked.

The firemen quickly began to rummage through the house room-by-room to search for any evidence of human remains. "There is no one home, thank God!" said the fireman.

"Thank you, Lord," said Mr. Davis. Mr. Davis began to walk around the property looking for some sign of us.

"We will be back in the morning to finish the investigation," said the fireman.

Shoot, they wouldn't do anything to Daddy if they saw him actually set the fire. Like I said, everybody knew everybody in this town, and nobody wanted to get in the way of Colby Winslow. Mr. Davis waved and thanked them for coming.

"Now, where are y'all, Marie?" we heard Mr. Davis call out.

CHAPTER 4

THE SHACK

THE MOON WAS DEFINITELY FULL THAT NIGHT, and it seemed to only get brighter after Mama prayed. Mama kept pushing us further into the woods as the commotion was going on, and she led us to an old brown, abandoned, tar-papered shack near a pond in the middle of nowhere. Mama said, "I used to live here when I was a little girl and fish in that pond everyday."

The shell of a house was very small and there were no windows and no doors. Folks around home always called places like that a "shot-gun shack." We didn't know it at the time, but we were walking into the next three years of our lives when we stepped up into that old shack. There were no rooms, and it was open all the way through from end-to-end.

Mama climbed up into the shack. "Come on, y'all," she softly said. "This is where we are gonna sleep tonight," she said. "It will be safe," she whispered.

We climbed up into the doorway one by one and lay down on the floor against the wall side by side.

I remember being amazed at how peaceful everything was there. The sound of the crickets chirping in the grass was such a sweet comfort to me. I felt like we were camping, and this place was our tent.

"Ouch!" said little Carol.

"What is it?" Stephen asked.

"The mosquitoes are toting me off," said Carol.

"Try to put your arms inside your shirt and maybe that will help," said Vern.

"They are eating me up, too," said Dan.

Swat! Swat! Swat! Every few seconds, you could hear the sound of one of us swatting those nasty vultures on our skin. It was awful being eaten alive by mosquitoes, but not as awful as being shot at and burned alive in our little house, I thought. Even with the popping noise going on all night long, as we fought those pests tirelessly, we were at peace. I could still smell the burning embers of the house in the distance, but I felt like I was a million miles away from the terror we'd just experienced. The brief moments of peace that I had hidden in my mind never lasted.

All of a sudden I heard the sound of a car. I began to fear it was Daddy, and he had found us again. It really didn't sound like Daddy's car, though. My heart started racing again, and we all huddled together in the corner as it came through the field towards the shack.

"That ain't Daddy's car," said Stephen.

"Mama, who could that be way out here?" Ron asked fearfully.

"Nikki, stay down," whispered Colby, Jr.

I kept popping up trying to see what kind of car it was. The car stopped right in front of the old shack with the headlights lighting up the night. Suddenly, the motor switched off, and we heard the door open and shut. The sound of footsteps grew louder and louder coming up the cement block into the shack.

"Mrs. Marie!" the voice said. "Are you here?" It was Mr. Davis, our landlord.

"Whew!" Carol said. "I thought it was Daddy again," she said.

Mama crept up off the floor in the corner and said, "Yes, Mr. Davis, it's me and the kids."

"What in the world are y'all doing out here, and what in tarnation happened to my house?" he asked. "Is Colby, Sr. with y'all?" Mr. Davis asked.

"No, sir," Mama said. "It's just us, and we aim on staying here in this place from now on, and I would like for you to give me your word that you will not tell a soul that we're here!" Mama said sternly.

"Marie, tell me what happened," Mr. Davis pleaded. Mr. Davis went out to his car and got a flashlight. He shined it in Mama's face, and saw the swelling, and noticed her black eye and bloody clothing. "Tell me, Mrs. Winslow, what happened tonight?" he asked.

Mama turned her head and told Mr. Davis, "He's drinking pretty hard tonight, and he accidently set the house on fire, I guess."

"I figured y'all were back here hiding from him," he said. "What about your face, Mrs. Winslow? Was that an accident, too?" Mr. Davis asked.

"Never mind all that, now," said Mama. "You just do what I asked you and don't let anybody know that we are here," Mama said.

"Can I do anything for y'all or bring you anything out here?" Mr. Davis asked.

"No sir, we will be just fine," Mama said.

"At least let me tell your folks y'all are here, Mrs. Winslow," said Mr. Davis. "They are gonna find out about the house fire, and I know they will be worried, if they drive by there and see it burned down, and they don't hear from y'all," he said.

"Alright," said Mama. "You can tell my Mama but that is all, and I mean it." Mama said.

"Well, I own all this land, and this here shack," said Mr. Davis. "I reckon y'all can stay here rent free as long as y'all need to, but you know there ain't no electricity and no running water here. What are you gonna do about that?" asked Mr. Davis. "Shoot, there ain't even a darn door or window; you can't stay here with all them young'uns!" he exclaimed.

"We will be just fine," Mama said. "Just you never mind!" she stated.

"Alright, but I am going to go right now and tell your folks," he said.

Pop and Grannie were Mama's mother and step-father who lived a few miles from us. They were hard-working people, living on fixed incomes in a single wide trailer, and they definitely didn't have enough room for all of us! Mama never asked them for anything. Grannie would always ask Mama if there was anything we needed and Mama would always tell her we were fine. We needed lots of things, but Mama never worried her folks for anything. She knew they couldn't support themselves and her whole family, so she didn't even bother to ask. Mama taught us to be extremely loyal to our own burdens. "Keep it to ourselves and keep trying to make things different," was her motto.

Grannie was such a special lady. She was very short in height, but she was fiery and strong. She was so kind and caring. I knew exactly where Mama had learned to love. Grannie was like a second Mama to each of us. She made us feel so special when we'd go to her house and never showed favoritism with any of us.

Pop was a short statured man but tough as nails. He was into horse trading and gardening, and he liked to hit the bottle on occasion. Grannie would tell us he would sometimes go off his rocker and re-live the war with the Japanese. I never saw him drunk a day in my life, but Grannie would sometimes tell us of the old days when he was drinking heavily. I remember Grannie talking about how Pop saddled up his horse and rode down to the community bar. That horse made many a trip down to Big T's bar and back. "It was a good thing the horse knew the way home because your Pop would get so drunk, he wouldn't know where he was!" Grannie said.

I never saw anything but normal when I was around my Pop and Grannie. That was something I was not familiar with at all. It was a welcomed sight, too. I loved going to Pop's and Grannie's house. It was some of the most peaceful moments of my childhood and peace was something I craved in my young life. We never talked about what was going on at home. We kept quiet about all of it. Pop and Grannie always had a garden with lots of good food growing and a milk cow, chickens, and horses on their small four-acre-farm. They taught us lots of great things about how to survive. I don't think they had any clue how bad things were at our house.

Mama kept everything to herself. She felt the responsibility of her choices in life and did not expect anyone to carry her burdens for her. Mama was raised with two half-brothers, named Bert and Jimmy, who were younger than her. Uncle Jimmy was killed in the Vietnam War. Mama was adopted by Pop when she was two-years-old. She never knew her biological father growing up and apparently Pop never let Mama forget that she wasn't his. She shared with us about how life was growing up with Pop back when he was drinking as to somehow give us hope that miracles can happen. She grew up in a violent household with Pop, so she was accustomed to violence and really didn't expect anything else from her husband either. Mama believed she was to stay with Daddy no matter what, and she also believed he would be and could be saved. She made me believe that, too but that belief was nowhere to be found that particular night.

As I heard Mr. Davis drive away through the field and down through the woods, I wondered if Pop and Grannie would come find us tonight. I thought maybe he would tell them, and they would come get all of us and take us to their house. It was late by this time, and I thought, if they didn't come tonight, they will surely come in the morning.

The mosquitoes kept on biting as the sweltering South Alabama heat poured over all of us like a bucket of water. Our clothes were drenched in sweat, and our hair looked as if we had just gone and taken a dive into that old pond. Mama use to say, if hell was anything like the humidity in Alabama, she was going to make sure we would all make it into heaven.

The sun came creeping up over the old shack the next morning, and I woke up swinging my fists as I always do. "I'm sorry, Mama," I said.

"That's alright, baby," she said. "Listen, we need to clean up in here and try to make it look half-way decent in case Pop and Grannie come by," Mama said.

I looked around at a shell of a house and I wondered how we could make it look good at all. There were old jars lying around inside, bird nests, and dilapidated old cabinets shoved in the corner. We got busy trying to clean it out. Stephen and Vern got some old branches from the tree outside and brought them in to Mama to sweep the floor.

Yes, this was going to be where we'd live and hide from Daddy. We were filled with excitement about living without the constant fear of being murdered each night. He could never find us here! He had no idea where we were. He thought he had done away with all of us in the fire. Nobody ever questioned him from the fire department or the law. He got away with arson just as he had gotten away with attempted murder of his wife and children multiple times before. We had moved many times trying to hide from him over the years but this time, he would not find us we thought!

As I took out the last jar from the floor, I heard a car coming across the field and into the woods. I ran so fast back inside and told Mama, "Somebody's coming, and I'm so scared!"

Mama had all of us hide in the corner again on the floor while she hid behind the tree outside in the yard. "It's Pop and Grannie, y'all," she yelled.

Yay! We all clapped and came running out. Pop had a '77 station wagon, and as he drove closer in the yard, I could see it was loaded to the gills with stuff. The car stopped, and Pop and Grannie got out.

"Marie," Grannie said. "What in the world, shug?" she asked.

Mama told Grannie, "We are fine, Mama."

"Well, you don't look so fine to me, let me see your face," she said.

"We've brought y'all some stuff you'll need to get by on, Marie," said Pop. Pop and Grannie had loaded that station wagon down with milk jugs full of water, vegetables from the garden, and a one-eyed Coleman stove that ran off kerosene for Mama to cook on. They had brought us an ice chest full of eggs and milk for breakfast the next morning. Thank God, school was now out for the summer, and we didn't have to worry about trying to make it there on time.

There were blankets, pillows, and an old yellow bucket with red letters written on it, filled with a broom, dustpan, bleach and a mop. It felt like Christmas in late May. There were washcloths, towels, and soap in an old basin that we could use for a sink; there were also toothpaste, toothbrushes, shampoo and a hairbrush.

There was a change of clothes for each one of us. I was so excited to see what they had brought us. It felt so good to have what we needed. The simple things mattered most to me. Pop pulled out a grill from the back of the car and rolled it up close to the shack. "Now, don't y'all put this too close to the house, it will burn it down in a heartbeat," he said. "I got y'all some charcoal and matches, too," he said. "I'm gonna bring y'all some of my chickens tomorrow so y'all can have a good supper," said Pop.

The chickens Pop spoke about weren't in a nice little package already cut–up; he was referring to his live chickens so that we could wring their necks and cook them. "Wringing a chicken's neck" is essentially snapping their neck to kill them in order to prepare them for a meal. Then, you have to pluck the chicken's feathers off before you clean them, and cut them up to cook them. It's all in the wrist. We had it down to a fine art. We had everything we needed now to set up housekeeping here.

We had no car, no money, no lights, no doors, no windows, and no running water, yet we were so happy! The serenity we experienced there was unlike anything we had ever known. We were content living in complete impoverished, primitive conditions because we were free from the violent threat we had faced for years.

I used to lie in the grass outside of the shack and stare up at the big, beautiful sky watching the clouds roll by and dream about the day when I could make life better for Mama. I felt such a calm, easy feeling when I did that. It took me away from the chaos we lived in, and I loved to write poetry and sing. My biggest dream was that I could make enough money one day to take care of my family, and we would never have to live like this again.

All of my siblings loved to sing except for Colby, Jr. He was "odd-man" out when it came to music. He could take it or leave it. Grannie loved to hear all of us sing. She made us feel like we were little stars, and if you ever went to visit her, she would talk your ears slap off your head about her grandchildren and how great they could sing! I remember one day when she and Pop came bringing us our weekly supplies, she brought us a big tape recorder that ran off batteries. She made us promise her that we would sit down and record her some singing.

Daddy had the most beautiful voice. When he sang, it was like he transformed into a completely different person. Mama had a beautiful voice as well, but she used to always give Daddy all the credit for handing down the talent to sing to us. It's like she wanted us to love him for something. She wanted us to think something good about him.

The summer dragged on and we would sit inside the shack and hit the record and play button on that tape recorder, and sing old gospel songs we'd learned in the Church of God with Mama back when we had a car to go places. Ron was our lead singer and Dan taught us how to harmonize. We made Grannie a nice, long cassette tape of all of us singing and gave it to her when she came back the next week. She was so happy. Mama said she told her that she played it for everybody who came over to brag on her grandchildren. She once even invited the Jehovah Witness folks come inside and sit down so she could play the tape for them. Traveling salesmen didn't have a choice in whether or not they wanted to hear us sing. Grannie would not even talk to them until they sat down in her house to listen to her grandchildren singing on her tape!

Singing was our way of escape from the reality we were living in. The truth was ugly, and we found our solace in music. I was especially driven by music. I didn't feel like I could make it without singing. As bad as things were, singing always made me feel happy inside. It was as if I was transported to another universe when I sang. I felt it so deep in my soul that I could not deny the healing power of a song. Music was my gift from God to soothe the pain that I was experiencing in my little world, and I knew it. I was so thankful I had something to focus on besides the truth.

CHAPTER 5
YELLOW BUCKET

W E SETTLED INTO THE DUCK POND SHACK QUICKLY, as we were no strangers to poverty anyway. The kerosene stove, with one burner, would fire off each morning, as we lay in a line against the wall on our blankets. We would listen as Mama would hum a little tune while she stirred a pot of vegetables, trying to make it go around enough for each of us. I remember the sweet sound of her prayers settling on the room for protection over her children. I remember her sobbing, as she cried out to God for our needs.

We had no bathroom or running water, so the yellow bucket with red letters on the side of it that Grannie had brought the broom in became our makeshift toilet. Mama placed it in the very corner of the shack just behind an old sheet she hung up for privacy with some bleach and a little water inside.

"Young'uns, this is all we got," she said. "Y'all need to take it out and dump it way out back and bury the contents when you get through going."

That yellow five-gallon bucket will forever be imbedded in my memory until the day I die. It was as if we had stepped back into the 1800's, and we were living like our ancestors did with their chamber pot (a pot kept under the bed to use the toilet at night). We wreaked of kerosene each day from the old lanterns Grannie brought to us that we used for a light source. If we got low on food before Pop and Grannie got back from week-to-week, we would go down to the Duck Pond and go fishing to have meat to eat. I used to think that old pond would never run out of fish. We'd catch a mess of 'em each time we went. God always gave us a plentiful mess each time we'd go fishing for supper.

Watermelon season came around, and the farmers in the field in the back of the shack were getting ready to prepare for the market. We raised enough money working in the field to buy our own school supplies and a suit or two of clothes each. Pop and Grannie loaded us up and drove us into town to go shopping.

I remember buying my first pair of Levi jeans that summer. I had just turned eight-years-old in May. I felt so proud of myself because I had earned those clothes with my own sweat. I had never been able to afford anything as nice as those pants before. It made me feel a little self-confident and strong. I would have at least one pair of decent pants to wear to school that would be equal to what the other kids were wearing.

School days were a comin', and we were not anxious about going at all. Grannie notified the school that we still lived at the same location as last year, but we lived deeper in the woods now. We would have to walk down the long trail through the woods to catch the bus each morning. That was all right with us because we didn't want anybody on that school bus to know that we lived in the shack by the Duck Pond! All the kids already knew we were one of the poorest families in the county. They could look at our no-name brand clothes and shoes and gather that information. "The clothes don't make the man," as they say.

Mama always taught us we were just as good as the next person, and Jesus loved us and died for us just as He did for the rich man. It was so hard to feel equal to the rich brats in school. We had manners, respect, and compassion for our fellow man, unlike our "equals" at school Mama talked about.

We had honor and ethics of kids twice our age, and we knew how survive the toughest of times by working hard and sticking to-gether. Nobody messed with one of the Winslow kids because you would have to fight the whole bunch of us. We took enough bully-ing at home that we were not going to take it off some punk kids! We were accustomed to fighting a game of survival with a "rag-ing bull" firing a gun (Daddy), so we were not afraid of anyone! We never started anything with anyone, but you can bet, we didn't dare back down from trouble when it came knocking!

CHAPTER 6
STRIKE THREE

I REMEMBER TRYING TO GET ALONG WITH ALMOST EVERYBODY at school. I was very good to all of my classmates. Some kids took my kindness as weakness, and they would "try me." It didn't take long before everyone knew there was something different about me. You just don't mess with stress. It will explode on you before you even realize it. I gave each person what I called "strike three." I could overlook the first time they messed with me and even forgive the second time, but if it happened three times in a row, it was on!

Janie Jones was a very well-clothed rich girl who noticed that I just so happened to wear the same Levi's to school about three times a week. She waited until the lunchroom was full one day to call me out on it. "Nikki, why do you wear the same clothes everyday?"

I just ignored her and shamefully put my head down and walked away. The lunchroom filled with laughter as I walked out. One morning, I was sitting at my desk during homeroom roll call, and Janie came at me again. "Nikki, your shoes are the same ones you've worn for the last two years in a row!" she laughed.

The entire class turned and focused on me and my feet, and the room began to roar with laughter. I quietly got up from my desk and walked calmly to the bathroom until the bell rang to change class. I was so humiliated. She waited until everyone could hear and focused on me just to ensure she could humiliate me. I had not done one single thing to deserve her attention. I truly wanted to remain invisible, but Janie kept calling me out in front of everyone. I had busted my behind in the fields to buy the clothes I had on my back, and I was proud of myself for that.

She continued to try to degrade me and put me down in front of others. What pleasure would that give a person? I could not fathom intentionally hurting another person for any reason. Why would she want to embarrass me? Lord, if she only knew where I lived, she would have a good time with that, I was sure of it! The second grade was becoming a social club, and I didn't like it.

I talked with Mama about the problem I was having at school with Janie and she said," Baby, she's just jealous of you."

I threw my head back and laughed out loud. "She's jealous of me?" I asked sarcastically. "What on earth have I got for her to be jealous of, Mama?" I asked.

Mama looked me right in the eye and said, "A loving heart!"

I really didn't understand that then, but the older I got I began to see what Mama meant. I didn't feel too loving on day three of the attack of Janie. I had been up all night fighting Colby, Jr. off me in the dark. I was mad, and not in the mood to be messed with by anybody else.

Janie came up to me in gym class as I was standing next to Johnny Raye, the cutest boy in school. Janie made sure Johnny Raye was never going to be interested in standing next to me again. "You got on those "Po-Boys" again today, Nikki," she laughed. "Can't your Mama buy you something decent to be seen in public in?"

My blood began to boil, my neck and face turned red as fire, and I hauled off and knocked Janie right square in the mouth. "Don't you ever talk about my Mama like that again, Janie," I said. Whop! Janie fell back onto the gym floor and I stood over her begging her to get back up so I could hit her again.

The whole gym really focused on me then. "Fight!" they screamed.

There wasn't anything left of the fight after I hit her. She began to cry as she was helped to her feet by her other rich friends. "You're crazy, Nikki!" she screamed.

Janie never bothered me again. I got talked about and teased about my out-of-style clothes, but I guarantee you, it was all done behind my back and through whispers from then on. The coach turned a blind eye that day. He knew I was singled out, but no one at school knew the whole truth.

The bell rang to change classes, and I walked outside the gym into the schoolyard. I heard a very familiar sound that I recognized well. It was Daddy's car. I was immediately overwhelmed with fear, as I looked up and saw him drive by the school. I couldn't tell anyone why I was shaking. I guess they all assumed it was because of the punch I just threw at Janie, but it wasn't. I was sorely afraid Daddy had come to pick me up from school. "What if he tried that?" I thought. I needed to tell somebody that I wasn't supposed to go with him. I sat in class the rest of the day so frightened he was going to be waiting for me after school. We were so loyal to our own hardships.

I didn't tell a soul. The last bell rang, and I picked up my books and ran as fast as I could to the bus line. I stood behind my brothers in line, shaking like a leaf.

"What's wrong with you, Nikki?" Ron asked.

"I saw Daddy drive by the school today during 4th period class change," I said.

"Don't worry about it, Nikki," said Dan. "He don't know where we are and he will never find us."

"Y'all just keep your mouths shut at school and don't tell nobody nothing!" Colby, Jr. said.

"I heard you got into a fight today, Nikki," Carol revealed.

The boys all started laughing. "What?" Stephen asked. "Who beat you up, Nikki?" he asked.

"Shut up, Stephen!" I yelled. "Ain't nobody beat me up and for your information, I laid her out!" I said.

"What happened today?" Vern asked. "Is that why you are so scared?" Vern asked.

"Y'all leave me alone, now," I said. "I've already told y'all I saw Daddy drive by the school and it scared me," I cried.

"Aw, come here," said Vern, as he hugged me lovingly. "I'm sorry I picked on you," he said. "It's gonna be alright, sis," he said.

The school bus pulled in, and we all climbed on board.

CHAPTER 7

THE TERROR OF HIDE AND SEEK

WE LIVED SO FAR OUT IN THE COUNTRY that we were usually the first ones picked up and the last ones to get off the bus each day. We sure didn't mind that because it left other kids in the dark about where we lived. Nobody asked us any questions, and they surely couldn't pick at the shack if they couldn't see it. It was too far from the road. It was another secret we were trying to keep from everyone else in order to stay alive.

It took him a few months, but Daddy eventually found us hiding out there in the old shack. He followed the school bus home the same evening I fought Janie. Daddy watched us get off by the road and walk down into the woods. Stephen spotted the old Ford Galaxy and said, "Y'all, it's Daddy! "Run!" he said.

We took off running into the woods down the trail to the shack. The school bus slowly pulled away, and we heard the distinct sound of that terrorizing motor quickly pull into the trail behind us. I began to cry with fear. My heart was pounding so fast inside my little chest that I thought I was going to die right then and there. We quickly jumped into the shack and warned Mama he was there.

"He found us, Mama!" Vern screamed.

"What are we going to do?" yelled Carol. Mama said a brief prayer, and we all braced for the worst.

The car door slammed as we huddled together inside near the corner of the shack. I felt as if the whole shack was shaking with fearful anticipation of what was about to come. What a time to have to go to the yellow bucket! I went behind the curtain and used the bathroom. My stomach was all in knots, and I finished up just as I heard Daddy yell, "Marie, I know y'all are here, so you might as well come on out of here and face me!"

I didn't have time to take the bucket out, and I was too afraid Daddy would get me if I did. "Pew-wee!" whispered Carol.

"I couldn't help it, Carol," I said. "I've been needin' to go to the bathroom ever since I got on the bus this evening," I said.

My focus turned back to Daddy quickly, as I heard him say, "I'm sorry I burned the house down like I did. I have changed, and I won't drink anymore, I promise. You just need to go on and forgive me so we can get past this," he said.

"Mama," I said, "please don't go out there."

"I don't believe him, Mama," Vern said.

"Marie, if you don't come out, I'm coming in," Daddy said.

"I forgive you," said Mama. "Now go on and leave us be," she said.

"No, h--- no! Now, you've got to let me see you a minute," said Daddy.

"Just go on and leave, now!" Mama said firmly. "We are doing fine right here without you, and I am tired and just want to be left alone with my children," Mama said.

"Who the h--- are you seeing?" Daddy yelled. "I'll kill that son of a bi---!" he screamed.

Mama was a very faithful wife and would not dream of complicating matters anymore than they were already. You couldn't convince Daddy of that, though. His own guilt made him mad with jealousy. She was a beautiful woman and could have her choice of any man. She had been faithful their entire marriage.

"Marie, I'm coming in!" he yelled.

Daddy started up the yard towards the shack, got one foot in the doorway, smelling like a moonshine still, and we all jumped him.

"Mama told you to just go on, Daddy," said Dan. "You ain't coming in here with us, now!" Dan shouted.

Daddy started punching and kicking all of us trying to get his hands on Mama. I saw Mama get up quickly and run to the corner of the shack behind the curtain where we use the yellow bucket. Mama grabbed the bucket and ran towards the front shouting, "Y'all move back young'uns!"

I was in disbelief as I saw Mama turned the bucket up and throw it on top of Daddy's head, as she shoved him into the yard. If I had known she was going to need that for a weapon, I would have tried to make it more lethal. The boys began to laugh so hard, and Carol was so grossed out she began to throw up.

"Mama, I'm so sorry I didn't have time to take it outside," I said.

"Baby, it's alright," she said. "I'll clean up this awful mess I made with it," she said.

I looked out in the yard, and Daddy was lying there motionless with that yellow bucket still on his head. "Maybe he's done passed out," said Colby, Jr. "I'll go out there and see," he said.

"No you won't," said Mama. "I'll go out there and see; y'all stay here," she said.

"Mama, please don't go out there, he will kill you!" said Vern.

"We will all go together, or none of us will go," said Dan.

Quietly, we all began to walk outside. "Mama, you might have drowned him," said Stephen.

"Hahaha," Mama laughed. "I think he's ok, but I'm not going to wake him up and ask right now," she said. "Let's all go back in. I've got some cleaning up to do," Mama said.

Daddy wasn't hurt in the fall. He was so drunk that he had passed out with the bucket on his head. Suddenly, our fear turned into resounding laughter, and we laughed so hard until we all cried. "Way to go, Mama," I said.

"I can't believe you did that, Mama," Vern said.

"Payback was a long time coming, wasn't it, Mama?" said Colby, Jr.

"Yeah, that's for all the times he has sh-- on you, Mama!" Stephen exclaimed.

"Hahahaha!" we all laughed together.

CHAPTER 8

CLOSE ENCOUNTER
WITH DEATH

NIGHTFALL SETTLED ON THE DUCK POND, and Daddy stayed out there in the same spot all night, snoring inside the bucket. The next morning I looked out and saw he was asleep inside his car. "Mama, I don't want to leave you today," I said.

"Yeah, can't we skip school today and stay here with you?" Ron asked.

"You might need us later on, Mama", said Dan.

"I guess I'll let y'all stay home today," Mama said.

I was so relieved! It was terrible not knowing what was happening at home when I was gone. The anxiety poured over me like a flood, and I could not concentrate on anything else. I heard the sound of a car door opening and I looked to see Daddy stumbling out of his car. "Marie!" he yelled. "Give me a bar of soap," he said. "I smell like sh--," he laughed.

Mama threw Daddy a bar of soap and told him he was welcome to use the Duck Pond, but he wasn't coming inside. I watched as Daddy walked down and jumped into the pond. The laughter of our night was fading fast, as he finished his bath that morning and headed back to the shack. "I need a da-- towel, Marie," he said.

Mama threw Daddy a towel in the yard, and he dried himself off. My stomach was like butterflies, as I anxiously waited to see what was next. Daddy got in his car and drove out of sight. For the moment, we were all right again. That was the greatest feeling in the world. Peace! What a sweet relief it was to know he was gone awhile longer. "He'll be back and we have to be ready for him," said Dan.

Daddy knew where we lived now, and it would not be long before he would "strong-arm" his way back into the shack with us. We cherished each peaceful second we had together. We would sit around and sing gospel songs all day long and pray those moments would last forever. However, we knew the "war" was not over, and we would have to endure until somebody got hurt, gave up, or got killed. Daddy was stubborn, and we all knew he was not giving up. Colby Winslow was not a quitter about anything! He had drive, determination, and stamina, and he was going to come back. It was just a matter of time.

A week passed, and I had settled into the false euphoria of our lives for a nanosecond to wake up with Daddy standing right in the doorway holding a shotgun. "Marie, I am coming back to stay with y'all!"

Mama sat straight up from her pallet on the floor in total fear. "Alright, Colby, come on in."

I felt as if my heart had ripped out of chest and fell on the floor. No way! I could not believe she gave up so easily. I guess she was afraid he would begin to shoot all of us, so she caved and let him come in. The boys didn't have a chance to even react. He was inside before they could even get up off the floor.

"Y'all ain't even gonna speak to your ole Daddy?" he asked. "I love y'all, and I promise I will try to do right by y'all this time".

I wanted to believe that so badly, but I knew what his promises amounted to. I yearned for peace already, and he had just walked into the shack. "Y'all get up and go outside and let me and your Mama have a minute to talk in private," Daddy said.

Nobody moved. Paralyzed with fear, I sat glued to the wall. What was he going to do when we left? Was today the day he would kill our precious Mama with the shotgun? I instantly knew my heart had not fallen on the floor as I felt it had because it began beating inside my chest as if I were running a marathon. What should we do? Should we get up like he told us to and go outside and leave Mama alone with him? He threatened multiple times to kill her if she left him again. Would this be that day? I began to pray silently and Daddy started walking towards us holding the shotgun.

"I told y'all to get up, go outside, and give us a minute to talk in private!" he yelled. "Are y'all deaf AND dumb?" he asked. "Now git!" he screamed.

We scurried outside like little mice running from a hungry cat. Colby, Jr. circled around back so he could listen out for Mama. Me and Carol were sitting in the dirt out on the east side of the shack as I began to hear Daddy's voice progressively get louder and louder. "You should give me another chance, Marie!" he screamed. "I told you I won't hurt y'all anymore!" he yelled.

Oh, sounded really convincing to me. (Sarcasm). Yes, sounding like he has done quite a bit of changing since he nearly burned us all alive. HA! All of a sudden, I heard stumbling and the all too familiar sound of fists landing against skin.

"Y'all, he's jumping on her!" I yelled.

"Come on!" Vern screamed.

As I began to stand up from the dirt, the shotgun blasted. Before I could get all the way up on my feet, I felt the shot pellets run through the very top of the hair on my little head. Frozen with fear, I began to shake uncontrollably. Did he just kill my Mama? I let out a blood curdling scream, "Mama! Answer me!"

The boys all piled into the shack on top of Daddy, as he and Mama were still wrestling over the shotgun. I continued to shake. It felt as if time had stood still, and I was living in slow-motion. I could not move, just standing there like an idiot. I needed to get with it and go on inside and check on Mama.

Daddy had pulled the gun on Mama, and she tried to push it off her when it went off and blew a huge hole in the wall of the shack. The blast of the pellets came zooming out exactly where I was about to stand up in the yard. If I had stood up a split second sooner, I would not have a head, and you would not be reading this account of terror.

Carol was still sitting on the ground at my feet. My next thought was to check on my baby sister. "Are you alright, Carol?" I asked.

Carol was sobbing, "I'm ok," she cried.

I could hear the boys fighting with Daddy as profanities spewed from his mouth out into the yard where I stood. I then heard the sweetest voice I had ever heard. It was Mama and I knew then that she was alive! I grabbed Carol and hugged her tightly saying, "Let's just wait until it's over, and we will go back inside".

I began to pray for peace to sweep through the shack and knock Daddy out. Yes, I believed God could tame the wildest beast, and I prayed for Him to slay this one in the name of Jesus. I was so relieved when the boys came out to find me and Carol. "He's out like a light!" said Vern. Hahaha.

"Are y'all alright, Nikki?" asked Dan.

"Yes," I said. "He about blew my head off," I whispered.

"What are you talking about?" asked Dan. "Come here and let me take a look at you," he said. The pellets had grazed my scalp and just did break the skin slightly.

"I'm ok, Dan," I insisted. "How is Mama?" I asked.

"Y'all come on in and help us pull him out into the yard before he wakes up," said Colby, Jr.

The process of preparing to study wild animals is quite simple. You shoot the unsuspected animal with a medicine-filled dart first that harmlessly puts the animal to sleep. The trick is, you've got to do all of your studying very quickly before the animal wakes back up and bites your head off. The same process happened with Daddy when he passed out. Yes, it had to be done very quickly or might lose an arm, leg, or your life. It was an extremely frightful process.

"Don't wake up the bear!" said Stephen.

"Ron, just take him on down to the car," said Mama. "When he wakes up, maybe he will go on and leave," she said.

"Mama, what are we going to do?" asked Carol.

"I don't know, baby," Mama said.

CHAPTER 9

YOU CAN'T STOP CRAZY

A S THE SUN BEGAN TO SET AND THE "BEAR" BEGAN TO SNORE, little Carol had more questions for Mama.

"Why don't you divorce him?" Carol asked.

"Baby, it's not that easy," Mama explained. "Just because you divorce a person, don't mean they will leave you alone," Mama said.

We had heard about divorce at school from some of our classmates whose parents were divorced, and sometimes we would beg Mama to divorce Daddy as if that would solve the violence once and for all. Ha! What a laugh! I'll bet we packed up and moved over a 100 times all over that small county. He would always find us and bully his way back in, and let me tell you, we thought the beatings couldn't get any worse, but when he caught back up to her, it was ten times worse than the time before because she left him.

Don't you dare judge my Mama! I have grown so exhausted of the question, "Why didn't she just leave?" Honey, she tried! Over and over and over again she tried! Back in the 70's in small town

U.S.A., there were no homeless shelters, no battered women and children "hide-outs," and nowhere for her to run with a house full of children in tow.

Everybody has solutions to the problems until they have walked a mile in those shoes. She didn't have the money it would cost for a divorce, and that would not have stopped him anyway. She was his "property," and she was going to stay and live with him in misery for the rest of her life if he had anything to do with it. If she wanted to leave, he would just kill her!

The equally unpleasant question has been brought to me numerous times, as well. "Why didn't she just call the law?" Ha! The whole town was afraid of him! The sheriff went to high school with him, and the deputies would shake at the sight of him. Many times they were called to our home by "concerned" neighbors who heard a commotion going on, but the law would not even attempt to make an arrest because of their own fear of him. We were on our own, and we knew it!

He was Jeckle & Hyde. Nicknamed "Superman" by many who had experienced or witnessed his supernatural, physical strength, he was well-respected as a man of integrity and strong work ethic by those he worked for around town. Those who really knew the truth were few, but those who did know, would not cross him no matter what, not even to save a woman and her children from being nearly killed each night in a violent rage. This was a cross that we had to bear alone, but not without God. God was the only one who really knew what went on in our lives.

I prayed to my heavenly Father each night for peace and sobriety for Daddy and for the molestation I endured at the hands of my own brother to stop. I struggled with hatred. I knew from all of the church services I had attended over the years that hatred was not pleasing unto God. It was so hard not to hate, be bitter, or despise with everything that was going on around me. I tried not to allow myself to feel those emotions so I buried them very deeply into my soul. I just pretended I did not feel that way and I tried to paint on a smile.

Reality is harsh, and a painted-on smile is fake. My true feelings about the chaos that I experienced would continue to be buried, and it would be decades before I could speak the truth, but right now, I simply had to survive. Survival for my family and me was my main objective and most important goal. There would come a day when I could express those darkest feelings but for now, I would suppress them.

CHAPTER 10

THE YEAR OF PEACE

G OD WAS SO GOOD TO US WHILE WE WERE IN THE SHACK. We made it through sweltering heat and nippy, fall-like winters while we were there. I remember the last "winter" we were there was actually unseasonably warm, and we walked around barefoot all-year-round. Daddy was back and settled in with us whether we liked it or not.

He let Mama take us to church on Wednesdays and Sundays. We attended the Church of God way out in the middle of nowhere in a small town called Frisco City, Alabama. The songs from the red back Hymnal still ring in my ears. Every chance we'd get, we would attend church there. I remember Mama telling me I began to sing at the age of two in that church. My older brothers and Carol and me were the "special" singers each time we would go.

Pastor Dewey Cox loved all of us kids and prayed hard for our Daddy to find the Lord. Brother Cox was a fire-breathing dragon of a preacher! He preached hell so hot you could feel your feet burn on the floor of that old church. Back then, there was no "children's church." You simply stayed in there with the grown-ups and they raised you on the Word! I am so thankful I was allowed to stay on the pew and learn. I was captivated by the power of the Holy Spirit as it moved through the room. I could feel the wind of peace and calm, and I craved it from the top of my head to the soles of my feet. Peace! Sweet peace! The Comforter (Holy Spirit) brought me the greatest solitude I had ever known in the midst of the wretched turmoil I experienced at home. I had an understanding of the Word of God at an early age mostly because of Mama's patient, loving ways of teaching me. She shared most of the stories from the Bible that I had heard Brother Cox share during his sermons, and it kept my attention. I hung onto every word, and I learned to apply it to my life on a daily basis. I learned to pray, believe, and have faith.

We had a prayer box at the front of the church, and each service Pastor Cox would ask if we had anyone's name we would like to put in the box to please come forward. I would always write Daddy's name down and take it to the front to drop it in. I did that for years. Revival was coming and I just knew, if Daddy would come with us, surely he would get saved. There was not one thing on earth I wanted more than to see my Daddy saved. Every time I knelt at the altar I prayed for Daddy's soul.

I was filled with excitement as the Evangelist arrived at our church. The first night, I was so thrilled to hear his message about forgiveness even for the drunkard. Wow! Daddy sure needed to be hearing this. I went home all smiles and hoped I could share some of it with Daddy before he got too drunk. Too late! He was waiting on the steps of the shack when we got home, fussin' and cussin' at Mama for being late. I knew a fight would ensue and I just braced for the "next round".

"Marie, who did you sit with at this church of yours?" Daddy asked harshly.

Mama calmly replied, "I sat with our children, and I wish my husband had been there with me, too".

"Well, what did y'all talk about or what did the preacher say?" Daddy asked.

Mama turned to Daddy and said, "Why don't you just come with us tomorrow night and find out?"

Daddy shoved Mama in the corner and shouted, "Don't you get smart with me or I will bash your brains in right here!"

Mama had the look of disgust on her face and said, "Go ahead and I will be free!"

"What are you talking about, Marie?" Daddy shouted.

"I'm talking about heaven and Jesus!" Mama screamed.

Daddy quickly turned loose of Mama and walked outside. It was calm and quite, and I was so scared that he was out there preparing to kill us, but he never came in again that night. Early the next morning, I thought I heard a familiar voice singing in the yard. It was Daddy. What on earth? Is he drunk already this morning? He couldn't be in a good mood. That was not possible. What is going on?

I stayed clear of Daddy that day, and later that evening when it was time to go back to the church, he cranked up the car and raced the motor. Oh no! He's not going to let us go back to church tonight. "Mama, what is he doing?" I asked.

Mama walked out to the car to speak to him. I could not hear their conversation, and that was suspicious because I always heard the unbearable profanities Daddy shouted at Mama. Mama came walking back up inside the shack with tears streaming down her face. "Mama, what's wrong, what did he do to you?" asked Stephen.

"Nothing, y'all," Mama said. "Y'all go get in the car and let's go to church," she said.

"Mama, Daddy's still sitting in the car," I whispered.

"Yes, he is!" Mama shouted happily.

"Mama, do you mean that Daddy is going to church?" Vern asked.

"Yes, Vern, that's exactly what I mean!" Mama said.

We could not believe what we were hearing. I quickly remembered what Pastor Cox said last Sunday about the devil going to church. I couldn't help but think about Daddy sitting up in there acting like the devil. I was so scared and happy and in total disbelief. I just knew he wasn't going for the right reason. He was so jealous of Mama. I remember one evening he came home from work drunk and caught her looking out the front window. She was peeking out of the curtains as she heard him drive up. He came inside and immediately beat her down in the floor for opening the curtains. I could not believe he even allowed us to go to church, and tonight he was going with us. I was in total shock.

Nobody made one single sound all the way to the church in the backseat of the car. When we arrived, the preacher met us at the door with hugs and a handshake for Mama and Daddy. "I'm so glad you came tonight, Colby," Brother Cox said. "Your old friend, James, has been asking about you," he said.

Brother James Mettis, the evangelist for the week, just so happened to be one of Daddy's old friends. Brother Mettis was saved and delivered from alcohol several years ago and here he was in our little country church the very same night Daddy decided to go with us. I knew that had to be God. Mama always told us Daddy was raised in the Pentecostal church. When he was a little boy, his grandmother would take him to all of the services. I had a hard time believing the monster I knew as my Daddy could have ever stepped inside of a church, but I was now witnessing a miracle this very night.

Daddy walked in and sat us all down on the back row. Brother Mettis was nowhere to be found until after the service started. He came out from the back like a cannon! He was a man blazing the way for the lost. He began to preach, and I immediately began to pray that Daddy was listening. The Holy Spirit began to move so powerfully strong through the room. Brother Mettis asked that every head be bowed, and every eye closed, and he gave the altar call.

I felt the pew began to shake, and I opened my eyes to witness in total surprise as Daddy got up and headed towards the back door. Oh no! He can't go out now. I continued to watch as he stopped at the back door and turned back toward the very front of the church. I was so worried about Brother Mettis. What did he say that made Daddy mad? I watched in horror as Daddy made his way to the altar. Much to my relief, I saw a raging lion become a gentle lamb right before my eyes. I could not believe what was happening. My Daddy was kneeling at an altar of prayer and crying out to God! Every one of us was crying and overwhelmed by what we were seeing.

Daddy came up a brand new man that night. God answered my prayers. Finally, there was peace at home for the very first time. Is this real? I must be dreaming. He had lots of proving to do to his family, co-workers, and friends. Nobody believed it was true. We decided we would enjoy it while it lasted.

He moved us all out of the shack and into a small, country house in Grove Hill, Alabama in the same county. We were so excited to have running water and electricity again! A fresh, new start was what we all needed. Was it possible that we had left the dreadful, conditions of the shack and the domestic violence behind all in one move? No more violence? No more gunshots? No more choke holds? No more alcoholic rages? I was ecstatic and very cautious at the same time. We settled into our new place renting from the sweetest ole lady named Mrs. Evans. She was a Godly lady who was mighty proud to offer her rental property to a hard-working man trying to support his family.

Daddy's newfound relationship with God was real. He would read the Bible, pray, and study each day. Word got around town to all of his drinking buddies. They could not accept ole Colby was giving up drinking. At least two men per week would stop by the house offering Daddy a beer. He held on strong and firm for one year and then…the year of peace came to an end.

CHAPTER 11

REMEMBERING YOUTH CAMP

DADDY RETURNED TO HIS OLD WAYS, BUT MAMA NEVER QUIT TAKING US TO CHURCH. I was turning twelve- years-old this year, and I was so excited about getting the chance to go to Youth Camp.

We got very involved with the youth at church and began to help out with fund raisers such as car washes, bake sales, and fish fry events to raise money for Youth Camp. Youth Camp was a week of young, Christian fellowship and revival for the church held each year at the Church of God campground. Mama promised me I could go this year if I worked hard and raised enough money to pay my way. I did raise enough money, and the time was drawing near for me to go.

This would be my first time away from Mama for a whole week. Daddy told Mama he would take me and drop me off at the campground. Mama wanted to make sure I got there safely, so she made my brother, Dan, come to look after me. Mama prayed for my safety and helped me finish packing my bags. She kissed and hugged me and Dan and waved as Daddy drove away with us. He promised

Mama he would not drink a drop until he got back home. Shoot! We stopped at every bar and tavern from South Alabama all the way up to the campground. Daddy made me and Dan wait in the car, as he would go inside and drink until he was full. Dan clutched me so tightly and kept telling me everything was going to be alright.

I was so scared sitting in the car watching the other drunken men come out, staggering to their cars. "We're never gonna make it to the campground, Dan!" I said.

"Shh, don't worry, Nikki," Dan whispered. "God is going to protect us," he said.

Daddy came out of the bar, loud and proud, cussin' up a storm, and daring every man in the parking lot for a fight. Me and Dan held each other tighter and began to pray for Daddy to calm back down. Daddy walked over to the car and peeked in the window and said, "There's my little young'uns, sitting there all quiet and shy."

Please don't call attention to us! We were trying to be invisible and just make it to church camp. Finally, Daddy hopped into the car and fired it up. With the engine revving and racing, he squalled out of the parking lot. I felt my heart begin to skip a beat.

"Darlin', why don't you scoot over here and drive this thing?" Daddy asked.

Shaking with fear, I said, "I don't want to Daddy."

Dan yelled, "Leave her alone, Daddy; you are scaring her to death."

Daddy pulled off the road and pulled me into the driver's seat as he went around to the passenger side where Dan was seated. "Slide over, you scrawny son of a b----!" Daddy yelled. "Now, I want you to drive this car, Nikki!" Daddy screamed.

I could barely see over the steering wheel of that old Ford Galaxy, and my hands were shaking uncontrollably. I was so terrified of wrecking his car. I gripped the wheel so tightly my knuckles turned white, as I pulled onto the highway. I had dreams my first experience driving a car was to be a pleasant experience, not like this. I put my foot on the gas pedal, and Daddy reached over and pushed on the top of my knee, holding my leg down as to make me go faster and faster. I reached speeds up to 70 miles-per- hour on an unfamiliar highway. "Please stop this, Daddy!" I pleaded. "I'm going to wreck and we might get killed!" I screamed.

Daddy threw his head back and laughed so hard. Dan was boiling mad, and he started trying to move Daddy's hand off my knee.

"Stop it, Daddy!" Dan said. "She's a little girl and she is scared!" he yelled.

Dan did distract Daddy long enough for me to get the car safely off the road, but Daddy's attention immediately turned to him, and they began to fight. I put the car in park and grabbed Dan by the arm, as we slid out of the driver's side door. "Get y'all's little a---- back in this car right now!" Daddy said.

"Not until you leave us alone," Dan said.

"Just get back in the car!" Daddy screamed.

Me and Dan walked around to the passenger side of the car, and Daddy slid over to drive again. I didn't know what was worse-- a 12-year-old being forced to drive at high rates of speed, or a drunk, raving maniac driving two kids into a tree or another oncoming car. I just kept praying we would make it there alive.

It was getting late, and I was supposed to be at camp that morning to check in.

We finally made it to the campground just as the sun began to set. Dan walked with me up to the window to sign in. Daddy sat in the car with the motor racing. I was so scared for Dan. He had to go all the way back home with Daddy in that car. "Please Lord, be with Dan as he heads back home tonight," I prayed.

Dan kissed me on the cheek and gave me a hug. "I sure hope you have a good time, Nikki," he said.

"How can I?" I asked. "I'm worried about all of y'all," I said. "Please send me a postcard to let me know you got home alright, Dan," I said.

"We will be back to pick you up next Saturday morning," said Dan.

I stood there in fear watching Daddy pull away with Dan. "Lord send your Angels," I prayed once more.

The camp advisor was a young lady from our home church named Hope, so I was glad I knew at least someone there. Hope walked me down to my cabin to meet the other girls. "What took you so long to get here today, Nikki?" Hope asked.

"We had a little trouble getting here," I said.

The feeling of excitement I had before I left home vanished when I got into the car with Daddy. I could not relax enough to enjoy this time away. I had worked so hard to make this possible, but my mind would not release that feeling of dread and fear. All I could think about was Dan getting home safely.

Hope introduced me to all of my roommates in my cabin. I quickly made friends with the other girls. It was nearly time for lights out, and I had just got unpacked. I put on my gown and said a prayer once again for Dan. I climbed into my bunk and quietly cried myself to sleep that night.

The week was filled with fun and games of all sorts. It could have been one of the most enjoyable times of my childhood. I tried so hard to allow myself to relax and be a kid. No matter how I tried, I still felt the stress of our reality at home. The services were action packed, spirit-filled, and the only strength I had to make it through the week. There were swimming, canoeing, and sports of all kinds to participate in. I found myself alone more times than not praying in the corner for our situation. Most of the kids thought I was weird. I guess I did appear that way to most of them. I had so many grown-up things on my mind. I didn't have time to play. I felt guilty for having fun at all, so I withdrew many times during the week.

It was Saturday morning, and I packed up all my things and went to the front where all the parents were lined up to pick up their children from camp. I sat patiently in a chair by the window looking down the road for Daddy's car. I watched as girls hugged, shared addresses with one another, and promised to keep in touch.

Some kids actually got emotional as they said their "good-byes" until next summer. One by one, parents would appear at the entrance and come in to claim their children.

Hope stopped by to speak to me before I left. She gave me a big hug and said, "I'm so glad you got to come this year, Nikki." She was helping all the kids connect with their parents at the entrance and directing traffic.

An hour went by, and there was only three kids left in the foyer. I was one of them, and a brother and sister, Chris and Janet, were still waiting on their parent's arrival. "I just got a phone call from your Mom, Janet," Hope said. "She said they had a flat tire and will be here shortly. "Nikki, I haven't heard anything from your parents," Hope said.

Oh no! I wonder what in the world has happened to Dan. Did he even make it home last week? I never received a post card from him. I quietly began to cry. I looked around as Chris and Janet's Mama finally arrived. I was the only child left in the foyer now. It was nearly noon, and Hope had still not heard one single word from my parents. We didn't have a phone at home. Daddy knew I was supposed to check out on Saturday morning, and he wasn't here. I was about to burst with anxiety. The boys advisor, Steve, came over to lock the gate and realized Hope and I were still there. "What in the world are you still doing here?" Steve asked.

"I haven't heard a word from her parents and she doesn't have a home phone," said Hope.

Steve smiled and came to sit down beside me and said, "Well, we will just sit here and wait with her."

Steve reached up and wiped my tears with his t-shirt. He made me feel so much better for a second or two. "My Aunt Rhonda has a phone," I said. I gave Hope the number, and she went into the office to try to contact her. Aunt Rhonda lived about 15 miles from our house, but I thought maybe she could ease my mind a little bit. If something was wrong, I knew she would have heard by now.

Hope called Aunt Rhonda and came back to the front where Steve and I were sitting. "She said she would drive over to Nikki's house to talk to her Mama, and then she would call us back," said Hope.

Steve drove down to the local fast food place and ordered us lunch. I hated to be rude, but I could not eat all of my food. My stomach was so nervous, and I had butterflies. Around 1:00 p.m., the office phone rang and it was Aunt Rhonda. She explained to Hope that Mama told her Daddy and Dan left early this morning to pick me up. I ran into the bathroom and threw up. Hope came in behind me, washed my face, and held me in her arms to comfort me as I cried. What has happened to Dan? I was so sick with worry now.

Hope brought me back into the foyer and told me to lie down on the couch. She brought over a blanket and covered me up with it. I cried myself to sleep. When I woke up, I overheard Hope and Steve talking about the situation. "What are we going to do?" Hope asked.

"We can't leave with her, because just as soon as we do, they are sure to come pulling up looking for her," said Steve.

"I don't know, but we can't stay here all night long," said Hope.

I sat up on the couch and looked out the window to see the sun setting on the horizon. Tears began to flow once more, as I had the sense of dread in my heart for Dan. Just in that instant, I heard the screeching noise of tires on the pavement. It was Daddy and Dan. Daddy sent Dan in to get me.

"We were so worried about you," said Hope.

"She has been crying and upset," said Steve.

Dan grabbed my suitcase and started out the door, holding me by the hand. "Thank you for sitting with her," said Dan. "I'm so sorry y'all had to wait on us," he said.

What was he going to say? What could he say? Daddy was slobbering drunk again, and we got here as soon as we could? There was no explanation just an apology as always.

Dan threw my suitcase in the back, and we climbed into the car with Daddy. At last, we were on our way home!

It looks like we are going to have just as much fun going home as we did coming to camp. I was beyond consolable. Shaking with anxiety, I braced myself for the ride home. We had not even made it out of town when Daddy pulled into the first bar. "I'll be back in a second," Daddy said. He slammed the car door and almost fell, as he opened the door to the bar.

"Dan, I was so worried about you," I cried.

"I'm alright, Nikki," Dan said. "We've just got to pray we make it home," he said. "He stopped at every bar on the way back up here again," Dan explained. "If he leaves the car keys in the car at the next stop, Nikki, we are going to leave him here," said Dan. "Mama has got to be worried to death about us by now," he said.

"Yeah, I know. I had them call Aunt Rhonda to check on y'all, and she went over to talk to Mama, too," I said.

Another hour went by, and we waited anxiously in the car. Daddy came stumbling out and got back into the car with a porcelain Indian doll for me, and a pocket knife for Dan. "I got y'all something," Daddy said sheepishly.

Dan rolled his eyes and took the knife out of Daddy's hand. I reached for the beautiful doll, holding it to my chest with a half-hearted smile for Daddy to see. "What?" Daddy yelled, "Y'all don't like it?"

"Yes, sir," I said.

"Thank you, Daddy!" Dan said, "Thank you, but this don't make up for the hell you've put us through trying to get home!" "Just get us home!" Dan pleaded.

"You ungrateful bast----!" Daddy yelled. "Give me that knife back!" Daddy screamed.

Dan took the knife and slammed it back into Daddy's hands. Daddy cursed and beat on the dash the rest of the ride home, but at least he didn't stop at another bar! Mama was sitting on the porch praying when we pulled up. Daddy walked up the steps and passed right out on the porch. Thank God, we made it home safe, but only by the protection of God's holy angels! I will never forget Youth Camp!

CHAPTER 12
NOT SO HAPPY BIRTHDAY

EARLY ONE EVENING AS WE DID OUR DAILY CHORES of feeding the chickens and gathering eggs, I heard the distinct sound of the bell. Mama had an old cow bell that she would ring that would call us in for supper.

It was so nice to be in Grove Hill in our new place. There were shrubs lining the concrete walkway leading up to the front door. It was a very small, white-framed house, with only two bedrooms, but we didn't care. We had lights, running water, and our little house was bright and picturesque compared to the shack. We had an actual toilet that would flush, and a beautiful, lush, green yard. Anything would have been better than the shack, and we were mighty proud to be crammed into that little place. We felt like we were living in a mansion. I was no longer embarrassed for anyone at school to see where I lived.

Since we had been in Grove Hill, I had actually made a new friend on the school bus named Linsey Cosgrove. Linsey had a great sense of humor, and I loved to laugh at the jokes she would tell on the ride to school. She had the same birthday as mine and we were turning 13-years-old Friday. On the ride to school, she invited me to her party on Friday night. I could barely contain my excitement. I tried so hard not to act like a total goofball, and I told her I would have to ask my parents. I was about to burst inside. I had never been invited anywhere. My excitement turned straight into caution. I wondered if she was just asking me to have me there and then make fun of me in front of everyone for not having the nicest clothes, or for being the poorest one in the school. I still couldn't help being excited, but my life had taught me to protect myself, also.

As I sat down at the table for supper, I was so glad that Daddy had not made it home yet. Now, I had the chance to ask Mama if I could go to Linsey's house on Friday night. After we said the blessing on the food, I paused for a moment and took a big, deep breath and said, "Mama, what would you say if I asked you to let me go to a party on Friday night?"

Mama looked puzzled and asked, "Baby, what kind party are you talking about?"

I told Mama all about Linsey and how we had become friends on the bus since we'd moved. "She's real nice, Mama," I said. "She's a good girl," I added.

"I'll have to ask your Daddy when he gets home," Mama said.

Oh no! It was over. I just knew Daddy would not be sober when he got home and I still would not know what to tell Linsey. What would he think about me going to a party? I had no idea what he would say and how he would act. I was so afraid, and I wished right then and there that I had never even brought the subject up to Mama.

After supper, I got up and helped clear the table and wash the dishes. I had the sinking feeling this night was not going to end well. Standing at the sink, I saw the old Ford Galaxy turn into the driveway. Daddy was home. My heart became to beat out of my chest. How was I going to ask this unapproachable, cruel, mean man if I could go to a party? Forget it! I would just tell Linsey that I was not allowed to go and save myself the punishment for even asking. I ran to Mama and said, "I really don't want to go, Mama. You don't have to ask him". Mama gave me a hug and kissed my cheek. She didn't say a word.

I watched from the kitchen window, as Daddy got out of the car to come inside. Each step he took up the walkway made my heart pound even more. "I couldn't get my check cashed this evening, Marie," Daddy said. "They paid me a day early but I got off work too late, and the bank had already closed," Daddy said. "Take it with you in the morning and go buy groceries so you can cash it for me."

What on earth? Daddy was actually sober on a Thursday night? I heard Mama begin to talk to him in a very soft and tender voice. "Nikki has been invited to a little birthday party tomorrow in town," said Mama. "Do you think you might allow her to go?" Mama asked.

"Ain't tomorrow her birthday?" Daddy asked.

"Yes," Mama said, "But her friend at school is having a birthday, too, and she has invited Nikki to come tomorrow," Mama said.

I listened closely as Daddy began to take off his work boots and throw them against the wall. "You are going to turn her into a little whore, ain't you, Marie?" Daddy yelled. Daddy screamed my name,

"NIKKI!" he yelled. "Get your little a— out here right now and ask me yourself!"

I was so shaken, crying, and so terribly embarrassed that I had even brought it up to Mama at all. "I really don't want to go, Daddy," I said.

"Tell me all about this so-called party you are planning to go to," he yelled.

"It's alright, Daddy," I said humbly. "I really don't want to go to it," I said.

"H--- yes, you do," Daddy yelled. "I said tell me about it right now!" he screamed.

Daddy was scary when he was drunk but he was also scary the very rare occasions he was sober, too. I began to tell Daddy through my tears all about Linsey and who her parents were and where she lived. All of a sudden, Daddy slapped me on the back and said, "Yes, I reckon I will let you go."

I felt as if I were a servant bowing before my master, as I backed out of the room with my head down, thanking him over, and over for his approval. I had no idea what humiliation awaited me the next night. I was so afraid he would change his mind before the time came, and I half-way expected him to, but he didn't. I was to ride the school bus home with Linsey that afternoon with all the other girls, and Daddy would pick me up at 11:00 p.m. when the party was over.

I had never been to a birthday party before. I almost felt as if the party was being thrown for me, too, as it was also my birthday.

It made me feel special to be invited. I began to pretend it was my party. Linsey treated me nicely, and she had not invited me there to make fun of me at all. She really did like me as a friend. I felt so relieved by that. I helped Linsey's Mama set the table with snacks, and Linsey went over to the stereo and started playing music. "Is this a dance party?" I asked.

"Of course," said Linsey. "I've invited all the cute guys from school tonight," she said. "Who are you going to dance with?" she asked.

I had never been to a dance, and the Church of God was totally against dancing, wearing make-up, or even pants at the time. I was nervous, but I was also so excited about being there and meeting all the other kids that I tried not to think about doing anything wrong. I was trying to relax and fit in. The party was held outdoors under the moonlight.

As the guests began to arrive, I noticed a certain young man named Mike leaning up against the wall. Mike had been staring at me since he got to the party. Linsey's Mama kept playing records of groups that I didn't recognize but I liked what I was hearing, particularly a group called *Alabama*. Mike began to walk towards me, and my knees began to shake. Could he really be walking towards me to ask ME to dance? I was floored. There was no way he wanted to dance with me, I thought. Mike was 15, and he couldn't possibly be interested in me. I turned my head in disbelief, as he took my hand and asked, "Don't you want to dance, Nikki?" I melted right then and there.

He treated me so softly and gently on the dance floor once we started dancing. We danced each and every song for nearly two hours. I was smitten. I never had anyone pay me any attention.

Mike held my hand and walked me into the dark behind the house for my very first kiss. I was instantly in love. I didn't understand what was happening until....Mike decided to run his hand underneath my shirt. I clocked him right in the mouth! I laid him out behind Linsey's house, and I ran as fast as I could back to the front where all of the other kids were still dancing. I was ready to go. Nobody was going to touch me like that without permission! I was not that kind of girl.

Mike dusted himself off and ran back around to the front begging my forgiveness. I was mad; I could not believe he tried that with me so soon. I wasn't totally oblivious. I know what young men do, but I was not going to be used up like that by anyone else to get a cheap thrill. I had fought so hard for my innocence, and I meant I was going to keep on fighting for it if I had to. Mike apologized many times throughout the rest of the night, and I finally accepted his apology.

I was standing under the porch light talking with Mike as I heard the Galaxy 500 coming around the corner. V-v-v-room! V-v-v-room! It was Daddy. The music filled the night sky as Daddy slid up to the curb to pick me up early. It was only 9:30 PM and the sun had just set. I watched in terror as he cut off the car, opened the door, and staggered up the driveway yelling, "Get your whorey a— into the car right now!"

Oh my God! If he had only known how brave I had just been as Mike made a pass at me. If he had only known I was a good girl, and I had not done anything to shame him this night.

The party became silent as my classmates watched in total shock, as he dragged me out of there by my hair, pushing and shoving me into the car while calling me the biggest slut in the world. I felt so ashamed and so dreadfully embarrassed. How could I ever face those kids again? My own father had called me a whore and a worthless slut in front of everyone. I was far from any of those things. I knew that, but they didn't. If my own father felt that way about me, how could I expect anyone else to feel any different? Mike and I knew the truth. If someone will just ask him, surely he will tell them what happened behind the house. Or would he? I was done, right there! I was done with social events for the entire high school existence.

I suddenly remembered when Dan tried to play football in high school a few years back. Daddy showed up drunk to one of his first games and went down to the actual field. Running full speed, he tackled Dan on the field in front of everyone present that awful night. Dan never played another game. He hung up his helmet forever.

I tried to tune out all the profanity Daddy screamed at me on the way home. Slapping me around and bashing my head into the dash made him impossible to completely ignore. I was forever in his mind a whore. I danced, wore pants, and I had even put on some of Linsey's lip gloss that night before the party started. I was destined for hell, although, the man telling me all of these things was so drunk he was swerving all over the road. I wanted to just crawl into a hole and die. I certainly did not want to ever step foot back in that high school again. I was now the freshmen whore!

We finally made it home, and Daddy shoved me all the way inside, yelling and screaming the whole way in. I cried all the way and cried even harder when we got home, as Daddy began to fuss at Mama for allowing me to go. "It's all your fault, Marie!" he yelled. "You are raising us a straight whore!" he screamed. "She was dancing and wearing make-up and hanging all over every boy there!"

he yelled. "You need your a—beat for letting her go to something like that," he said. "Come here!" Daddy yelled.

Daddy began to hit Mama over and over backing her into the corner until he got tired. Mama just stood there and took it that night. The boys were already in bed asleep when I got home but they quickly sprung into action. Daddy had already stopped hitting her by the time they got up, though, and then he left.

I cried and cried as I felt Mama's beating this time was all my fault. "I am so sorry, Mama," I cried. "I won't ever ask to go to anything like that again, Mama, I promise!" I exclaimed. "I didn't know there was going to be dancing there, Mama," I said.

"It's ok, baby," Mama said softly. "I hope you had a good time, Nikki," she said.

I couldn't bear to tell Mama what happened when Daddy arrived to pick me up. I just knew that was the very first and very last party I would ever attend, and it was. I became a social introvert from then on. What a not-so-happy way to ease into adolescence!

CHAPTER 13

DEMONIC SWINE

W E DIDN'T STAY MUCH LONGER IN GROVE HILL. Mrs. Evans was a kind old soul, but she wanted and needed her rent money just like everyone else. Daddy's rages had literally destroyed her little white house. It wasn't the neat little home it was when we moved in. There were holes in nearly every wall, doors knocked off the hinges, and window panes broken out of the living room. It was time to pack up and move again.

We found a very old farmhouse in Frisco City, Alabama for rent. It had thirteen rooms, high ceilings, fireplaces in every room, and a porch that wrapped all the way around the house. But, in typical Winslow fashion, this house was sitting right in the middle of a hog farm. We were now living with pigs. The house was built in the 1800's, and it was surrounded by a fence. Just outside of the fence was a hog farm that belonged to the landlord, Mr. Ted Tredwick. Mr. Tredwick rented this place to Daddy for $65.00 per month.

Colby, Jr. had graduated, left home, married, and joined the military. I was so relieved! Dan had just graduated high school the year before, and Ron was a senior this year. Ron, Vern, Stephen,

Me, and Carol all still went to school. The house was plenty big for all of us. It was just another possible embarrassment, as it sat in the middle of a hog farm. I knew when folks on the school bus came to pick us up it was going to be bad. I tried to make the best of it.

We moved in, got settled, and immediately things started happening there that could not be explained. We would hear noises on the front porch like footsteps with no one there, hear doors opening and closing, with everyone in one room, and those blasted pigs were pure evil.

Each morning when we walked outside of the fence to catch the bus, the pigs would chase us. There was a rope tied to a huge oak tree limb near the fence. The pigs would literally seethe with anger, as they watched us through the fence, just waiting for us to come out to catch the bus. We started grabbing the rope, and one by one and we'd swing up and over the fence and hit the ground running out of the pig yard as fast as we could. The boys always went first as to give us girls a little distraction and advantage. It was extremely hard coming back into the pig yard trying to make it back inside the fenced home. We came up with all sorts of diversions like throwing rocks, food, or any other thing we could to make the pigs leave us alone.

I remembered a story from the Bible when Jesus cast out the demons, and they went into the pigs that ran off the cliff, and all died. I wish these pigs had run off a cliff.

Once we got home, things carried on as usual with violence filling our nights with horror. Something was definitely different about this house. Not only were the pigs pure evil, this house had some spiritual force that was anything but good. The very ground that surrounded the house seemed to ooze with a bad presence.

I remember coming home on a midsummer's evening to find a fire raging in each of the thirteen fireplaces in the house. My first thought was that one of my brothers was playing a joke on us. One by one, we all denied having anything to do with setting the fires, as we pitched in to put them all out. I got such an awkward feeling that day. I just prayed for God to protect us. For a while, things calmed down, and no one heard strange noises, but it wasn't very long before even crazier things began to happen.

Ron awoke to a small, demonic figure dancing around the foot of his bed. As he grabbed his shotgun off the wall, it disappeared from sight. Vern had a mysterious room that was not connected to the rest of the house. You had to go outside to get to it. One night, he was awakened by a shadowy figure that came through his window and attacked him. He physically fought this figure. As he began to pray, he watched as the figure left the room out through the fan in the window. Mama was walking down the hallway one evening, and a strong, powerful force attacked her from behind. It jumped on her back, forcing her to the floor. As she began to speak "in the name of Jesus," the force released her and let her go. We were all being attacked the first year we lived there, but we didn't share or compare stories until things got really bad.

Daddy thrived in this house. His beatings became more severe, and his drinking got heavier than ever before. He was completely taken over. I will never forget when the Lord sent a preacher to save Mama from certain death. Daddy had taken Mama down the hallway to talk with her in private. He grabbed her by the neck and began to physically choke the life out of her. She was alone with him as we were all in the kitchen. Just before Mama went unconscious, there was a knock at the front door. It was a visiting preacher. Daddy opened the door, and Mama was able to get up on her feet and run to the kitchen. We took off out the back door that night and left him with the preacher.

By the time we came back home, Daddy had left for the night. We had no idea he was choking her until we saw bruises on her neck. He had started attacking her in silent as to prevent us from jumping him. We would have to be more on guard now than ever before. Mama moved in the room with me and Carol, so she could lock Daddy out at night. That just made things worse for her, but she stood strong and decided she needed some rest after the last episode. He nearly killed her for sure that night before the preacher knocked.

One evening, Daddy came in drunk earlier than usual. Dan was home waiting on us to get home off the bus. Daddy started punching Mama in the face, and Dan stepped in to counter-attack. Daddy and Dan were pretty evenly matched by this point. Dan was a strong, young man around 20-years-of age. The fight carried over into the front yard, and on out into the ditch near the road. Mama tried to play referee and stop them, but things escalated into an all out-and-out brawl. Dan started getting the best of the old man, so Daddy picked up an ax handle and crashed Dan on the side of the head with it. Dan was knocked out cold for more than five minutes, according to Mama.

As all of our luck would have it, just as Mama picked up the ax handle and commenced to beating Daddy to the ground with it, the school bus full of unsuspecting children and adolescents arrived at our driveway to drop the Winslow's off for the day. Oh what joy! There were questions like, "What is your Mama doing to your Daddy? Who is that passed out in the yard?"

Laughter resounded throughout the bus that evening, as we held our heads in shame at the events unfolding right in front of our peers. Just a typical day at our house, but we surely weren't ready to share that with the whole school. We stopped Mama just shy of killing Daddy that evening.

"Mama, what on earth has happened?" I asked.

"I jumped him after he hurt Dan," Mama said.

We didn't know it then, but this is the very day we lost Dan as we knew him. The incident caused a traumatic brain injury that he would never get over. Dan would never be the same again. Daddy finally woke up. He was battered, bruised, and bleeding, as he limped away down the road. Peace for the night.

CHAPTER 14

DAN'S SICKNESS

THINGS BEGAN TO TRANSFORM IN DAN after the incident with the ax handle. We started noticing changes in Dan's behavior, his mood swings, and personality differences. He began to talk to himself, laugh out loud inappropriately, and claim he was biblical characters. It was so hard to watch this transformation in my dear brother. He was always right there to comfort me in my times of trouble and fear. I just wished that I could do something for him now that his mind had gone astray. What could we do? We prayed and pretended everything was alright for years, but things got worse.

Dan would leave the house at night, and we would have to go search for him. One day, Dan stood outside on a small throw rug with a bible in his hand, preaching so loud he lost his voice. We tried to reason with him and coax him back inside. It was so hot; we were worried he would dehydrate. That night, Dan slept on that little rug. When morning came, he got up and came inside.

Daddy had been gone for several days now, so we were blessed not to have him adding stress to the household at this time. Dan's condition just worsened it seemed by the day. We felt frustrated, confused, and in shock about his recent onset of delirium. It was extremely hard on Mama. She was determined she would keep him at home and not even think about hospitalization.

The worst became even worse! One evening, during the dead of winter, Dan began his preaching spell and went into Mama's closet and put on her white skirt and white shirt. He had convinced himself he was Michael the Archangel, and he was headed out the front door to go baptize people in the pond down the road. Mama called for each of us to come and help hold him down to remove the clothing, so he would not have to suffer any humiliation from the neighbors. Dan was strong, and it literally took each one of us sitting on him on the couch to remove that skirt. He was convinced this was his robe of white. We could not contain him. He began wandering up and down the roads each day, laughing out loud, mumbling, and sometimes singing. It broke my heart.

Things got increasingly worse while we were living at the Tredwick farmhouse. It was the perfect residence for the devil to finish destroying our family. The place itself was pure evil. The pigs, the unexplained forces we had seen and heard, were straight out of a horror film. I remembered from scripture that Satan was *"like a roaring lion seeking whom he may devour". (1 Peter 5:8 KJV).* The preacher once said he preyed on the weak in body and mind, and our strongest battles are fought in our minds.

Dan was so sick and getting sicker mentally each day that passed in that horrible place. I was so afraid if we didn't get out of that house that somebody was going to die this time. Mama was feeling the same way, and I will never forget when she announced we would be moving closer to Pop and Grannie. "Y'all listen," Mama said, "I know it's been very hard to stay here, and y'all have been scared many times, but I have found us a small house near Pop and Grannie. We will start moving out soon."

"Yes!"Vern yelled.

"I'm so excited I could turn a cartwheel," I snickered. Me and Carol held hands and danced around in a circle laughing, jumping, and squealing like young girls do.

We drove into town on Ron's truck to gather up boxes from the back of the Piggly Wiggly and I.G.A. grocery stores, so we could start packing right away. On the ride home, Mama took us by to see the "new" place she had rented from Velma Dotom. The Tredwick house was cold, dark, and spooky, but we had plenty of room for all of us there. The new house Mama had rented was all of two small bedrooms and one bathroom. It was bigger than the shack and had electricity and a small fireplace in the living room and even had wall heaters. We were only one mile from our beloved grandparents! We were so excited and filled with anticipation to get back home and start packing those boxes.

The boys quickly began to load furniture on the back of Ron's truck and haul it on over to the new place. Carol and I started rumbling through our dresser drawers for things we wanted to keep and things we wanted to throw away. That didn't take long; we didn't have anything of any value. It took several days for the move to be completed and I remember on the very last load, the Tredwick house caught on fire. The living room was filled with smoke and we desperately distinguished the fire. Mama said, "We are leaving this house and whatever demon is still living here can have it! "In the name of Jesus, you can not harm me or my babies any longer!" Mama shouted.

We peeled out of that yard so fast it made the old demonic pigs stop and take notice. Daddy was left scratching his head wondering where we had gone again. It wouldn't take him long to find us. We got settled into our new little place and I was turning 14 in May. I felt as if I were 41 and had lived a lifetime already with everything we had been through and experienced so far.

I had hoped that moving again would be helpful to Dan's state of mind, but it wasn't. The damage had already been done and it was beginning to intensify. One day, when Ron came home from work, the front door was locked. Dan was inside and would not open the door for Ron. Ron called out to Dan over and over but Dan would not open the door.

Dan yelled, "Get thee behind me Satan; go away and leave from here!" Dan screamed.

"But Dan, it's me, Ron!" Ron exclaimed. "Open the door up so I can come inside; I'm your brother," Ron said.

Dan suddenly flung open the front door, grabbed Ron's body, lifting it over his head, and threw him off the porch into the yard yelling, "You are Satan, and you have to go!"

Thankfully, Ron was not hurt during this fall. Mama came pulling up in the yard from work and asked, "What is going on?"

Seeing Mama almost triggered reality for Dan. He calmed down and sat on the porch. Ron got up and brushed himself off and took Mama inside. "Mama, we have got to do something for Dan, because somebody is going to end up getting hurt," Ron said. "What if that had been you or one of the girls?" Ron asked.

Mama sobbed silently with tears streaming down her face and said, "I know, son; I just don't know what or how to do anything about it," she cried.

It was plain to see Dan needed treatment, but Mama was bound and determined to keep him at home as long as she possibly could. The neighbors began complaining that Dan was scaring them the way he walked up and down the roads each day talking to himself and laughing uncontrollably.

We didn't know anything about traumatic brain injuries, but we did know that our brother was gone. We had lost him to a world of fantasy, delusions, and unrealistic imaginations.

Grannie began to put pressure on Mama to seek professional help for Dan. Mama was breaking into a million pieces. She just could not even think about having him placed in a psychiatric facility. We didn't have enough money to make ends meet, and we certainly didn't know how we were going to have him committed without any money. When you're poor, and you get sick, addicted, or depressed, you deal with it. We had no choice but to deal with it. We saw no quick cure or high dollar remedy available to use.

Grannie had been told the State of Alabama had a grant-funded Mental Hospital in Tuscaloosa called Brier Hospital. She finally convinced Mama to sign the papers to start the process. Mama cried for days. I truly believe it was the most gut-wrenching decision Mama had ever made in her life. She changed from that moment on. She no longer demonstrated that strength I witnessed as a younger child. I saw her crumble for the first time.

Dan got accepted to Brier Hospital and the local Sheriff's Department escorted him to the facility in Tuscaloosa. We would go and visit when we had enough money. That wasn't very often, so we wrote him letters each week to stay in touch and let him know how much we loved him. He would stay in and out of that mental facility for the rest of his short life.

CHAPTER 15

KANSAS CITY?

DADDY RESURFACED IN THE WOODS behind our new little house. He camped out there watching and lurking around to see if Mama had a boyfriend. Mama got a job at the textile plant in town. Now it was just Ron, Vern, Stephen, me, and Carol left at home with Mama. Junior was still in the military, had married, and started a family. Thank God that chapter of my life was over! I prayed for the protection of his children. Dan was in the mental hospital. Ron had just graduated high school and took a job welding, and Vern was now a senior in high school. Stephen, me, and Carol still had a few years to go.

Ron helped Mama with the bills for the household. He was a mighty good hunter and fisherman. If it weren't for his skills as an excellent outdoorsman, we would have starved to death. He kept the freezer stocked as much as he could with some kind of wild animal. He often took a plate to the woods for Daddy to eat, too. We all knew he was there. I guess the boys getting older and stronger finally slowed him down a little bit. They were strapping young men who inherited Daddy's supernatural strength, and as they grew, Daddy began to keep his distance a little more. He knew the boys were now strong enough to really give him a terrible fight, and he was getting older, too.

Mama was just plain beaten down by this point. I vowed I was going to get out on my own as soon as I could to lighten her load. She still had four of us in school to try and support on less than minimum wage. I took babysitting jobs every chance I could and worked after school many days helping local farmers during gathering season. I was now in high school and still a dreamer. "If only I could make it in the singing business," I thought. Why, I could buy Mama everything she ever needed and help all of my family live a better life. I grew up singing in church and knowing the right way, but in my adolescent years, I allowed someone to coax me into singing Country Music, and I slowly began to drift far away from church and God.

Carol and I joined a band with an older fellow Mama knew from school. His wife was a teacher, and they were a well- respected family in town. We became his backup singers, and Mama would let us ride on the old van to do "gigs" with them in the regional area. We made good money, and it would start the road to bigger dreams for me. All I wanted to do was sing. I had been bitten by the music bug! I didn't have a backup plan, and I certainly did not believe that college would ever be a part of my future. I knew we couldn't afford it. I had absolutely no other aspirations in mind whatsoever. I loved to run long distances and had always loved sports, but I had my heart and mind set on music.

I started working after school with Mama at the textile plant in town about the time I turned 15. A sophomore in high school, I was in the Future Farmers of America club and Chorus. I was approached by my instructor, Mr. Duke, about auditioning for the National Chorus. I went to my chorus teacher, Mrs. Swan, and she

helped me make a demo tape to send in for review. The National
FFA convention would be held in Kansas City, Missouri that year. I
was certain that I would not be picked since there were thousands
of entries from all across the United States. I just sang the song
and my teacher placed it in the mail for me.

A few weeks went by, and me, and Mama came pulling up in
the driveway at home after we got off work that evening. Mama
asked me to go check the mail. I walked down to the mailbox and
opened it to find the usual bills waiting, but there was a brown
package lying face down underneath the bills. I picked it up and
turned it over. It was addressed to me. It was from Kansas City,
Missouri. I didn't want to open the package, because I just knew
it would be a "Thank you for your recent audition, but you're not
good enough!" I was literally shaking in my shoes I was so nervous.
Even if I were to be picked to sing at the convention, there was no
way possible for me to afford to go!

I took a very deep breath and I slowly started opening the
package. I closed my eyes, as I slipped the letter out and it read,
"Congratulations!" I opened my eyes to see those words on the
paper, and I nearly fainted right there at the mailbox. There is no
way! I ran screaming up the driveway with the letter held high in
my hands. Mama just knew from the way I was screaming she had
another child to lose their mind. She came running out the front
door and asked, "Nikki, what on earth has got hold of you?"

I quickly handed the letter to Mama for her to finish reading it
to me. "Congratulations!" You have been chosen from thousands
of students from across America to come perform at the National
FFA Convention in Kansas City, Missouri!" the letter read. Not only
was I chosen from thousands of entries, but the letter went on to
inform us that I was the only person chosen from the whole entire

State of Alabama. I would represent my school, my county chapter, and the entire State of Alabama!

What? There must be some mistake! There is no way a Winslow child, one of the poorest children in the county, was going to represent the entire State of Alabama! That's impossible! Nothing good has ever happened to me. I just don't have these kinds of experiences. This was by far the biggest thing that had ever happened to me. I was excited, as Mama reminded me that I could do anything I set my mind to do. All of the excitement faded quickly, as I finished the rest of the letter. I was going to have to come up with money for a round trip airline ticket and expense money to stay in a fancy hotel in downtown Kansas City for a whole week. Mama looked at me with tears in her eyes and whispered, "I'm so sorry, baby."

"It's fine, Mama. I know I can't go, but it was just good to be picked!" I said.

I wadded up the letter and threw it on top of the table in the kitchen. I spent the rest of the evening outside crying in the backyard swing. I didn't want Mama to know how bad this hurt me. I stayed away from her so she wouldn't notice.

A few days went by and finally my instructor at school, Mr. Duke, asked me if I had heard anything from Missouri. I told him I was accepted. He was so excited and asked, "Why didn't you tell me?"

I bowed my head and mumbled, "I can't afford to go, Mr. Duke."

Mr. Duke lifted my chin up off my chest and looked me in the eye and said, "Yes, you can and yes, you will go!"

Mr. Duke asked me to bring the acceptance letter to school the next day, so he could see what all I needed. I was so embarrassed that he was asking to help me. I wanted to crawl up in a corner and die. I worked very hard, Mama worked very hard; we all did. We were not impoverished because we sat on our lazy behinds and drew welfare. We were impoverished in spite of the hard work we did each day.

The next morning, I got ready for school and tried to straighten out the acceptance letter. Mama kissed me on the forehead and said, "Maybe it will somehow work out, baby."

She was so hurt she couldn't afford to send me. I knew she was scheming in her head to see what bills she could possibly put off paying, so she could make this happen for me. I went in to see Mr. Duke that morning and took him the letter. When he got finished reading it, he was yelling, "YES!" Mr. Duke asked, "Do you know how big this is?"

Mr. Duke ran out of the office and took my letter to the principal. The principal called the newspaper, and they took my picture for the front page that morning. I was really embarrassed then! I still could not see how in the world I was going to be able to go. I didn't want the newspaper to do an article, and then I couldn't go. Mr. Duke asked me if he and his wife could drive me home that evening, so he could talk to Mama. They were a nice couple. I didn't understand why they wanted to talk to Mama, but we had the evening off at the textile plant, so I agreed to let them take me home.

Mama was starting supper when we got there. Mr. and Mrs. Duke and I went on inside and I announced that we had company. "I didn't hear the bus pull up, Nikki," Mama said.

I said, "Mama, I didn't ride the bus home; Mr. and Mrs. Duke wanted to bring me home, so they could talk with you about something."

Mama got a strange look on her face, as she invited them on into the living room. "Mrs. Winslow," said Mr. Duke, "We wanted to come ask you face-to-face if we could personally take Nikki around town to try and get her sponsors to go to Kansas City. We don't want to offend you in anyway, Mrs. Winslow," said Mr. Duke, "but she really needs to go," he said.

Mama thanked them for coming and told them she would have to think about it. Mr. and Mrs. Duke got up and shook Mama's hand and left. Mama took one look at me and my wide-eyed expression and said, "Nikki, I guess sponsorship would be your only way to go since we can't afford it."

The next day Mr. Duke asked me what Mama's decision was, and I told him she had agreed to allow me to try sponsorship. Mr. Duke screamed! "We will pick you up tomorrow and get started," he said.

CHAPTER 16

PRINCESS FOR A DAY

MR. AND MRS. DUKE CAME BY EARLY that Saturday morning to pick me up. I really didn't know what asking for sponsorship entailed. I was willing to go and at least try because I knew it was the only way I would be able attend the Convention.

We pulled into town and began making our way down Main Street. Mr. Duke stopped the car right in front of Damsel's Department store. I was terrified. I had never even been inside that store before. What on earth are we doing here?

Mrs. Duke got out, opened my door, and smiled at me. "Come on, Nikki," she said. "Let's go get you something pretty to wear on your trip."

I immediately put my head down with my eyes fixed on the floor. I had no business in this store. When the door buzzer went off to indicate customers, the very distinguished lady looked down her nose in my direction. She looked me up and down, as if to let me know I was completely out of place here.

Mr. and Mrs. Duke greeted the "fancy" lady at the counter. "We are pleased to introduce you to Nikki Winslow," Mr. Duke said. "Miss Winslow will be representing our county, school, and the great state of Alabama at the National FFA Convention this year in Missouri!"

"Winslow?" the fancy lady asked. "Is this Colby and Marie's daughter?" she sneered.

"Why, yes, she is!" Mr. Duke proudly proclaimed. "We were hoping your store would be interested in sponsoring Nikki's trip in some way. We will be glad to mention your business name in the front page article the local newspaper is working on," said Mr. Duke.

"H-m-m-m," said the fancy lady. "I reckon so."

I just wanted to crawl under the floor. I was so embarrassed. I didn't need anything from this uppity snob! I would have never darkened the door of her highfalutin store. I was ready to go home already. Now the whole town would read about the Winslow girl begging to go somewhere. I was not happy.

Mrs. Duke asked, "Would you be willing to offer items of clothing for sponsorship?"

"Sure, pick her out three new outfits," said the fancy lady.

Mrs. Duke walked me back to the clothing racks and asked, "What size do you wear, Nikki?"

I deeply appreciated what Mr. and Mrs. Duke were trying to do for me. They were sincere in all of their efforts. They didn't pity me, or look down their nose at me like I didn't belong. They simply wanted to assist me in making a trip they both felt I had earned and deserved to experience. However, the "fancy" lady at the counter was only out to get her name in the paper for giving to charity, or at least that is how she made me feel each time she looked my way. I just knew she would drown if she walked outside in the rain.

I tried on the first three outfits without hesitation and quickly handed them to Mrs. Duke. "These fit just fine," I said. I was just ready to get out of there. I almost choked when I saw the price tag on each item. I had never spent that much on clothing in my lifetime! I was very proud of the clothes, and I thanked the lady at the counter on the way out. She just kept that same snarl on her face, as I walked out never to return to her store again.

The next stop was the local feed store. We walked in, and Mr. Duke introduced me to the owner, Mr. Black. "Oh, Lord, yes. I sure am proud of you, Miss Nikki," he said. "Ain't you Colby Winslow's daughter?" he asked.

"Yes, sir," I said.

"Me and Colby went to school together and he is much of a man!" Mr. Black said.

"Yes, sir," I said. How could I argue with his compliment of my Daddy? No one would believe what we had been through, so we just shook our head and agreed with the ones who thought they knew him best.

Mr. Black brought out his big checkbook and wrote me a check for one hundred dollars right there on the spot. I was blown away by this generosity, and I really felt it was a sincere gesture on his part.

"Thank you!" I shouted. I appreciate this so much, Mr. Black."

"You are plum welcome, Nikki, and please tell your Daddy I said hello," he said.

"I will," I said.

We walked back to the car and headed on down Main Street for another stop. Mr. and Mrs. Duke were so patient and kind to me the whole day. One store and then another, they took me in and spoke up for me until we had every cent of the money that was required to go to the convention including the airline ticket.

CHAPTER 17

WISE TO EVIL

WHEN THE TIME CAME FOR ME TO GO to Kansas City, I borrowed Grannie's suitcase and packed up all the pretty clothes and other items folks around town had donated to me. I kissed Mama, and she prayed for my safety. I had never been on an airplane before. I was frightened, but Mr. and Mrs. Duke drove me all the way to Birmingham to assist me and help me get on the right plane. We said our good-byes and off I went up the terminal gate to board the plane. I was beaming with excitement dressed in my FFA National Chorus jacket to represent our little town well.

I was seated across the aisle from a heavy set gentleman dressed in a fine looking suit and tie. He had diamond rings on his fingers and a gold watch on his wrist. He appeared to be an extremely wealthy man. I turned to him and gave him a nod and smile as a small gesture of greeting. He then proceeded to open his mouth and talk all the way to Kansas City as if to impress me and gain my trust. The hair on the back of my neck stood up many times during our conversation on that flight. I could not put my finger on it, but I knew something was not right about this man. He knew I was traveling alone and when the plane touched down in Missouri, he assisted me with my carry-on bag as we walked together down to the terminal gate. "Let me help you find your luggage, Nikki," he said.

I didn't want to be rude to the man, but I knew I had to shake him off my trail pretty fast. My gut was screaming to get as far away as I possibly could. I listened to my gut. My home life had taught me how to protect myself, and it also taught me not to trust anyone especially strangers. We walked on to the baggage claim area, and he claimed his bags and continued to stand there with me as mine came up.

How am I going to get rid of him? What does he want with me? I was afraid I already knew the answer to that question. "Come, let me drive you to your hotel so you won't have to try and flag down a cab, Nikki," he said.

"Uh, ok," I stuttered. I could yell and scream, but he hasn't done anything to me, yet. I could stomp his foot with my shoe, but he hasn't hurt me, yet. He put his arm on my shoulder, and that sent me over the edge. That's it! I will not die, get raped, or sold into slavery in Kansas City today! I suddenly stopped and said, "I left my other bag on the plane so you can go ahead without me."

"I will wait for you, darlin'," he said.

"No!" I shouted. "I will get my own cab and I am not going with you," I said.

I caught the attention of a security guard near the entrance. He came up and asked me if I needed help. "Yes, sir, can you just stand with me, and help me get a cab to my hotel?" I asked.

The stranger hurriedly made his exit out the front entrance. I stood shaking, and silently thanking God for his safety and protection on my life. I wasn't certain the stranger would have harmed me, but something way down deep told me to get away from him.

Life at home had prepared me to be ready and on-guard for anything at anytime. I had better be wise in a city like this. We had two red lights in our small town. Kansas City was bigger than any place I had ever seen. The kind security guard flagged down a cab for me and my journey to the hotel started. Zooming in and out of traffic was making me feel sick. I remember thinking the hotel should be closer than this. I began looking at the cab driver with suspicion. He was of Middle Eastern decent and wore a turban on his head. He had the blankest stare I had ever seen. It was as if he didn't have a soul. His eyes were empty.

We had been driving for at least 10 miles now, and it seemed as if we were driving out of the city. "How much longer?" I asked sternly.

"We are about to arrive," he stated, as he glared back at me in the mirror.

We topped the hill and there it was---the grandest hotel I had ever seen! Thank God I got here without being abducted, robbed, or raped. I really felt like I would go ballistic on someone if they tried anything like that with me. I just wanted to get in, get settled, and meet my roommates for the week. I tipped the cab driver and made my way inside for a week filled with some of the greatest memories I had ever experienced. I made friendships there that would last a lifetime. Knowing there is strength in numbers, I stayed close to my roommates the whole week as to stay safe.

The Dukes arrived back at the airport to drive me back home at the end of the week. I could not wait to get home and tell Mama all about my trip. I prayed everyone was safe at home. I was just glad to be going home to a dirt road.

CHAPTER 18
LYING IN WAIT

I SURE MISSED MY FAMILY while I was in Kansas City performing at the National FFA convention. I had them on my mind the entire week I was gone. I worried more about their safety than I did mine. I got settled back into the normal routine at home. Me and Mama got called back to work at the textile plant. A fast-paced job, we had to go in from 7:30 in the morning and work until 5:30 in the afternoon. School was out for the summer, and I was glad to have the much needed work again.

One bright June morning, I recall hearing Daddy's car crank up in the woods behind the house. Mama said they hadn't heard anything from him the entire week I was gone. "It sure has been eerily quiet," Mama said.

He was waiting for just the right time to make his move. Daddy found out exactly where me and Mama worked, and he followed us to town that day. "Mama, I can see him back there behind us," I said. "Why is he following us?"

"He won't try anything at the plant," Mama said.

We pulled on up in the parking lot of the plant, and Mama locked her doors. Grannie had given Mama an older model Plymouth to drive back and forth to work each day. It was a two-toned car with yellow and brown colors and it smoked like a freight train, but it got us where we needed to go.

Daddy came flying by the plant blowing his horn repeatedly. Me and Mama walked on into work and clocked in. We were very busy that day, and the workload was stressful. At lunch, I ran to clock out with Mama, so we could go grab us a bite to eat. Daddy's car was parked across the street. He was just sitting there lurking at us. "Mama, what is he doing?" I asked.

"I have no idea, baby," Mama said. "Just ignore him." We had our lunch and went back to work.

As the 5:30 buzzer sounded, I grabbed my time card and started towards the clock. I waited for Mama at the time clock. Standing there, I peeked out the entrance and saw Daddy's car still sitting there in the same place it was at lunch. Mama came to clock out, and I said, "Mama, he is still out there."

We hurried out into the parking lot, and I glanced over to Daddy's car. Daddy was not sitting in the car this time. I didn't see him anywhere. "Maybe the cops picked him up," Mama said. "Let's hurry up and go while he's gone."

Mama hopped in the car and unlocked the door for me. She placed the key into the ignition, and the car would not start. She tried and tried to crank the car with no luck. Most all of the other workers had left the premises, and it was just me and Mama left behind the gate. Mama got out and opened the hood. I got out with her to see if

I could help her. Suddenly, I heard footsteps running up behind us. It was Daddy! Oh no! My heart began to run away with me.

"What do you want, Colby?" Mama asked. He stopped running and the distinct aroma of alcohol drifted on up to my nostrils. I could smell him from 10 feet away.

"You are going to talk to me, Marie," Daddy demanded. "I took your battery cable off your car, so you would have to stand here and talk to me today."

"I have nothing to say to you, Colby," Mama said. "I told you I was tired, and you were not coming back this time."

Daddy leaned into Mama and grabbed her face as if to kiss her. Mama pushed his arms away and went back to try to tighten the battery cables on the car. "What are you doing here, you little slut?" Daddy asked.

"I work here with Mama," I said.

"Oh, y'all can't leave her alone anymore, can you?" You always got to be in my way, don't you?" Daddy said.

Mama got the cables back on, and I slid back into the car to try and crank it up. It worked! I slid back over into the passenger seat, and Mama ran to get back into the car, so we could leave. Daddy staggered around to the passenger side window and acted as if he were going to give me a hug. He leaned into the window and suddenly drew back his fist to begin punching Mama in the face. I was so enraged at what I was witnessing that I began to pound my fists into his head. "Drive, Mama!" I yelled.

Mama pulled the car into drive and spun out of the parking lot with Daddy holding onto the side of my door. I kept beating him in the head with my fists, but he wouldn't let go. Mama pulled onto the road, and I yelled to Mama, "He's still holding onto my door; you're going to kill him!"

I reached up with my mouth and bit his fingers, and he finally let go and rolled into the ditch. "I reckon he's alive, but I wouldn't suggest you go back to check because he's probably going to murder both of us for all that just happened!" I said.

I could see Daddy in the rearview mirror getting up out of the ditch and walking back to his car. "Yep," I said. He's gonna live to kill us another day, Mama, but not today."

We laughed at how ridiculous that sounded, but we both knew it was probably a true statement. Now he had started attacking her at work-- a public place. What was next? I'm just so glad I was with Mama that day. I'm not sure what would have happened if I had not been there to help fight him off.

When we got home, Stephen, Vern, Ron, and Carol were cleaning the yard. I ran up to Ron and told him what Mama and I had encountered with Daddy. "I'm sure glad you know how to take care of yourself," Ron said. "I sure hope he won't come down here and try to get back at you."

"Grab a rake and help us finish up," Vern said.

Mama went on inside to start supper, and I helped my siblings finish up the yard. Little did we know, that would be the last time we'd see Daddy for a while. He was offered a job with a construction company building department stores. He would move on to a town about 60 miles away, and it would be the last time he would terrorize Mama again.

CHAPTER 19
SAFE TO LEAVE

SINGING CONTINUED TO BE MY ONLY GOAL, and I just knew that was what I was born to do. School became more and more mundane and useless in my future plans.

I was planning my escape. I would not be a burden to Mama much longer if I had anything to do with it. She was worn out from the violence and trying to make ends meet so we could have the bare necessities.

I remember picking fruit from the pear trees and blackberry vines just to have something in our bellies. We tried to help all we could, just as we had always done, by using the money we earned to buy our own school clothes and school lunches. Vern met a young lady who me and Mama worked with and fell head over heels in love with her. Her name was Karen. Vern and Karen got married that summer and moved about 5 miles away from us. It was now safe for each one of us to spread our wings and fly out of the nest. Daddy was gone! Mama had peace she so deserved.

I met a young man that summer that promised me the moon, and I fell for it hook, line, and sinker! His name was Elliot Cambell. He had jet black hair, hazel eyes, and the most beautiful tanned skin from being outside each day. Elliot was a roofer. Oh no! A roofer! Roofing was not something I ever wanted to do again, but at least we had that in common. We seemed instantly connected, and we'd talk for hours about dreams and aspirations. He was a very talented wood craftsman. He could take an old piece of wood and make it into the most artistic creation your eyes have ever seen. I admired his talent, and he seemed to admire mine. I was smitten with this young man. I knew in my heart he was the one I would leave home with. We dated (which consisted of talking on the front porch) for several months, and Mama could tell something was different about this fellow. He won over the boys (my brothers) and Carol, too. He seemed so genuinely in love with me.

Elliot proposed to me on the front porch under the most beautiful, full Alabama moon. I accepted, and then I realized I had the tedious task of asking Mama. What was even scarier than that was the fact that I would have to tell my brothers. Daddy was gone. Junior was still away in the military. Vern and Karen were married. Ron, Stephen, and Carol and I, were the only ones still left at home with Mama. I told Elliot to stay away for a few days until the shock wore off. He drove away, and I went back inside.

Mama was sitting on the couch waiting for me to come in. "Nikki, what is it that you need to tell me?" she asked.

"Nothing, Mama," I said. "Come sit down and talk with me a while," Mama said gently.

"Mama, I want you to know that I have fallen deeply in love with Elliot, and I plan to spend the rest of my life with him!" I exclaimed. Tears began to roll down Mama's face as she looked down at her feet. I started to cry with her. We embraced, and Mama knew at that moment, I was going to leave with or without her permission.

"Nikki, you have always been a strong-spirited young lady, but that's just what you are, young," said Mama.

"Mama, I can take care of myself, and you know I can," I said.

"You're only sixteen-years-old, Nikki," she said. "You have a lot of living left to do before you need to get married and have kids."

"Mama, I feel like I'm forty-years old as much as we've been through in our lives, and I know without a doubt, I can make it on my own," I said.

"I just wanted so much better for you, Nikki, and I'm not talking about this young man in a negative way; I'm just saying that I wanted to you finish school and have a better life than we have had here," Mama cried.

"I give you my word I will finish school, Mama," I promised.

Mama never gave me an answer that night. She wouldn't even talk to me about the subject matter for nearly a week. She cried, and I cried, and we just held each other tightly. Elliot was planning on coming by that afternoon, and I was hoping Mama would talk to us about what she had decided. I heard the sound of his car pulling down the dirt road up to the house. "Mama, he's here," I yelled.

Mama came out on the front porch to greet Elliot and said, "Y'all come on back here to the swing and let's talk."

Elliot got out of the car and was visibly shaken. "It's alright, honey," I whispered.

"Now sit down," Mama said. "I've always known this child was strong, and I would have to let her go her own way," Mama said. "However, you need to listen closely to what I'm about to tell you, Elliot. She is still my child, and if you ever hurt her in any way...I will find you. This is how this deal will go, and I need you both to listen to me," she said. "She will finish school and not drop out for any reason or excuse," Mama stated.

"Yes, ma'am," said Elliot.

"I mean it!" Mama shouted. "I have worked my fingers to the bone trying to give them what they needed, and all I expect is that they finish school so they will have a fighting chance to stand on their own two feet!" Mama said. "Do you understand?" Mama asked.

"Yes, ma'am," Elliot said. "I..." said Elliot.

Mama stood over Elliot, pointing her finger shouting, "Just hush your mouth and listen to me! "If you ever feel the need to leave her, you had better not leave her stranded," Mama said. "She will always have a place to come home to, and if you EVER hit her...I WILL kill you!" Mama proclaimed.

Elliot sheepishly smiled and said, "I love her with all of my heart, and I will take good care of her, Mrs. Marie."

The courthouse wedding was planned for September. Mama had found another house that was bigger and cheaper on rent about two miles from Velma Dotom's house. We were going to have to move again. I was so thankful I was going to be leaving, so it would be one less mouth for Mama to feed.

I helped pack boxes one last time at Mama's and loaded them into Ron's truck. Carol was emotional about me leaving soon. My brothers were just plain mad at Mama. I spent as much time with all of them as I could. We talked and laughed and cried more than anything. I was going to miss my family terribly. I could not believe Mama would only have three left at home. I felt safe in going now more than ever, because we had made the move to the new rental home, and I knew it would take Daddy a long time to find them again.

CHAPTER 20

THE WEDDING

STEPHEN HAD JUST GRADUATED, and I was in the eleventh grade. Carol was a freshman. I remember walking into school that year feeling so distant and free. I was going to be married and still going to high school. I'm sure every kid there would automatically assume I was pregnant and I had to get married. It was August and September was coming! I didn't tell anyone at school. I just kept quiet and to myself, as I always did.

There was a very large refrigerator box sitting in the hallway at school near the front entrance. I soon learned the school was holding a food drive for a needy family in the county. Each student could bring a canned-good from home and receive extra credit in class. I walked by that box every morning going to my locker, and I watched as it progressively filled to the top with all different kinds of food. I saw the maintenance men at the school load the box up on a dolly and drive away with the box. When Carol and I got off the bus that evening, the box was sitting on the front porch. Wow! Were we voted the neediest family in the county? We were very thankful to have the food, and we definitely needed it. It sure was a bit embarrassing to think that someone was aware of our situation. As hard as we worked, we could never get ahead.

I was getting nervous and anxious about the wedding. We didn't have the money for the proper church wedding, and I was okay with that. I never had high expectations anyway. We would be just as married as anyone.

The day came quickly, and I wore my old boots and jeans to the courthouse. Dan and Junior couldn't make it, but all of my other siblings and Mama came to serve as witnesses to this event. We said "I do" and walked out of there married. No honeymoon plans were made; we couldn't afford it anyhow. My brothers helped my husband (that sounds weird) move all of my things into his little block house in the next county that evening. I was now Mrs. Nikki Winslow Cambell. Wow! Wow! Wow!

The next day I had to go to the school office to show my new marriage license and get my transfer to the new school. I walked into Mrs. Swan's room, and she began to cry. "Why are you leaving, Nikki?" she asked.

"I have moved, Mrs. Swan." I said.

"Is Carol going with you?" she asked. I explained to Mrs. Swan that I had moved out on my own and I didn't give her any further information.

Mr. Duke was very upset to see me go, too. He had been so good to me the years I had been in FFA. I was really going to miss him. "Are you pregnant, Nikki?" he asked. "Why on earth did you get married?" he whispered.

"You really don't understand, Mr. Duke," I said.

"I'm going to miss you," he said.

I walked out of my school for the last time and drove to the new school to get registered. I had every intention of keeping my promise to my Mama. No matter how embarrassing it would be for me, I was ready to meet the challenge and continue school just as I told her I would.

I was the "new kid" in school for the first time. No one knew me, and it felt nice not being well known. I was married, and rumors started flying around the school yard before too long. I stayed to myself as usual. I would catch the bus in front of our little house in the country and come home to start supper each evening.

CHAPTER 21
TROUBLE IN PARADISE

I WAS A GREAT WIFE who took care of her husband, managed housework, and schoolwork all together. I was adjusting to my new life like a pro. Elliot was roofing houses in the area with a local roofing company. I was happy and at peace with my new home life. I missed Mama and my siblings so much, but I was determined to show her that she had not made a mistake in her decision.

One evening, I got off the bus and made my way down the lane to our house. I could see Elliot's old Ford truck in the driveway. I wondered why he was home so early today. I opened up the door to go inside and found Elliot completely intoxicated! This is just not happening! My heart sank into my gut. Why? It was if I instantly knew I had made a huge mistake with this guy. This is who he really is. I was floored! Mortified! Disgusted!

I walked in, and Elliot came right towards me, staggering and trying to kiss me. "You're not going to kiss me right now!" I shouted.

"Why are you getting all hostile with me, baby?" Elliot slurred.

"Because you're drunk!" I yelled. "I will not live like this!" I screamed.

I walked outside to the front yard and cried. I was so hurt and let down. Disappointment filled my soul. I always vowed I would not live the way Mama had to live, and I would never stay in an abusive relationship. Look at this mess! This had better be a one-night event. I am not going to take this junk.

Standing outside in the yard, I could hear Elliot rumbling through the dresser drawer. We kept a loaded pistol in the top dresser. I thought about the gun briefly, but I really didn't think he would get it out. I turned back to the door to go inside, and the door was locked. This "turkey" has locked me out of the house! What in the world is going on? I began pounding on the door, calling out to Elliot, "Let me in!"

I stood outside beating on the door and trying to convince him to let me inside for at least ten minutes. I walked around to the living room window and tried it. It opened! Great. Now I could get in and try to calm him down. I lifted the window and began to climb inside when, all of a sudden, I felt the familiar chill of a gun barrel placed against my head. Oh my God! Not in this life, too. What have I done? Who is this person? What am I doing in this place?

Although I had lived a lifetime of training for this moment, I was completely caught off guard by this situation. I did what I would do at home. I began to pray out loud and ask God for His protection over my life. There is power in the name of Jesus!

As I spoke the last words of the prayer, "In Jesus' Holy name," Elliot laid the gun down, grabbed me, and held onto me crying saying, "Don't ever leave me again."

I stood there, frozen. I didn't say a word. I would have my say tomorrow. Elliot passed out on the couch, and I stayed up all night contemplating going back home to Mama's. I should have, but I didn't.

The next morning came, and he didn't even remember what he had done or said, but I quickly filled him in on every detail with precision. "Don't you ever, ever, EVER point another gun at me unless you intend to use it and never, ever, EVER lay your hands on me in a violent manner or I will kill you dead!" I screamed. "You have no idea what I have inside of me," I said. "You don't want to wake it up, either!"

CHAPTER 22

THE BEGINNING OF THE END

ELLIOT HAD PROMISED ME MANY THINGS in our life together. We were to move to Nashville, so I could pursue a career in Country Music, but for now, we were moving to Texas.

Texas? What in the world are we moving to Texas for? There had been many severe storms out near Dallas, and Elliot had tons of roofing jobs lined up out there. It would mean an increase in our income, and we so desperately needed that extra money.

Mama would be so hurt to hear this news. I sure didn't want to tell her. I would have to change schools again!

We settled outside of Dallas in a small apartment. Elliot had so many jobs lined up that he couldn't keep up with all of it. He began putting pressure on me to quit school and go to work with him. I kept remembering my promise to Mama. He just kept pressuring me until I finally caved in and quit. How stupid! Mama would be crushed. I must be nothing but a huge disappointment to her now and a liar, too. It took months for me to muster enough courage to tell her in a letter. I could only imagine how devastated she must be. I was still going to keep my promise, somehow and some way.

The next few years would mean moving and moving again-- Texas, Oklahoma, and finally, Tennessee. I was now in Nashville, and I could start working on my dream. I sang every chance I got in clubs and festivals, and I went to songwriter's events. I had some small success, but nothing like I had hoped for.

In September, Elliot got a call that his father had suddenly passed away, and his step-mother had not made an attempt to come for his sister, who was only twelve-years-old. She had basically abandoned little Ella, and by the time we could make the move back down to South Alabama, Ella had become a ward of the state. We had to do something! I convinced Elliot that we should fight for her and finish raising her to give her all that she needed. Ella was family, and where I came from, family stuck together. We petitioned the court for temporary custody, and after countless interviews and court dates, we were now considered Ella's permanent caretakers. I was so thankful she was allowed to rejoin her family, her brother. I could not imagine what it would be like if Carol were left without Mama, or our brothers to help her.

I was only 18-years-old, married, and now the caretaker to a 12-year-old girl. We instantly formed a bond that would never be broken. I was going to be the best I could be for this young lady. I prayed I could make the difference in her life that Mama had made in mine.

Things were going well for us now that we were back in Alabama. Elliot took a job in restaurant management, and at last, I was away from that blasted roofing! I could focus more on my music and songwriting when I wasn't waiting tables throughout the day.

Elliot started having difficulty sleeping at night, and I remember waking up many nights to find him carving his wood crafts in the wee hours of the morning. I remember thinking how this new job and new responsibility of Ella must be stressful for him. I took a weekend job singing in a local club to make extra money to help out with expenses for Ella. It was exhilarating to be performing each week on a regular basis, although I hated the environment of three to four hundred intoxicated listeners each night.

Ella had a sitter for several hours while I was gone, and Elliot would come with me to "watch" me. He became increasingly jealous and paranoid during this time in our marriage, and I would soon discover the exact reason for his staying up for days on end was not associated with stress at all. Elliot became addicted to crack cocaine.

How did this happen right under my nose? I watched as he destroyed everything we had worked so hard for. We purchased a small home, and he never made the first payment. We bought a car, and he put four brand new tires on it right before it was to be repossessed for his lack of payment. Our furniture was repossessed on my birthday that year and top of all of that, he turned in his job resignation at the restaurant. He was quitting. He was plotting his escape from us. He was going to leave us "holding the bag."

I could not understand how this could happen. What triggered this fall? I feared for Ella. She became afraid of him and his quick-tempered attitude. I would not stay in this situation with this child. I began to save tip money and the money I made from singing so that Ella and I could move out on our own. Ella came to me one day and said, "Nikki, if you ever leave Elliot, can I please stay with you?"

117

"Yes, you certainly can, Ella." I said. "You can stay with me as long as you want to; I love you!" I explained. I hugged Ella and re-assured her she was always safe with me.

CHAPTER 23

DREAM OF PREPARATION

D RIVING HOME FROM THE RESTAURANT one afternoon on our street, I noticed a group of men working with shovels in the ditch. One man stood out to me with such great intensity that I had to stop the car and turn around. I drove back by the group of men and much to my surprise, it was Daddy! I was shocked to see him only one block from my house. His hair was gray. We had not heard from him in four years. I often wondered if he was even still alive. It was surreal to actually see him standing there in front of me.

I parked the car and started walking up to him. "Daddy?" I asked.

"Oh, Nikki!" he said. "It's so good to see you, darlin'!"

A world of mixed emotions poured over me and instantly, I remembered the last time we shared some family "time together." It was extremely ironic that he was only one block from me working. We hugged briefly, and I told him where we lived. I told him I had married and was raising my sister-in-law, Ella. Daddy was staying in the work trailer two streets over, and he said this job would last for several weeks. I left and told him I would try and come by again to see him later in the week.

I couldn't rest that night. There was something significant in the fact that out of nowhere, he had appeared almost in my yard. I wondered if he was still drinking, but I didn't want to ask.

I slowly drifted off to sleep, and I so vividly remember dreaming of a great and terrible fire. I could see the fire blazing in the distance, and as I walked closer up the dirt road, I could tell it was Grannie's house. The fire was not all consuming. It was only burning the ends of the trailer in the rooms where Grannie lived on one end, and Dan stayed on the other when he was home. I ran furiously towards the blaze, but the crowd kept pushing me back telling me not to come any closer. I could not do anything to save them. The ends of the trailer fell onto the ground in a pile of ashes.

I woke up sweating profusely. I sat straight up in the bed, and I began to weep. The very next day, Grannie lost her battle to cancer and died in Mama's arms. Carol made the drive to pick up Dan from the mental facility to come for Grannie's funeral. It was a beautiful tribute to a Godly little woman who loved the Lord and loved her family with all of her heart.

It was wonderful to see Dan and get to talk with him for a while. After the funeral, we were all standing outside in Grannie's yard. Dan was standing about 50 feet from me, and he immediately made eye contact with me. He rushed over to me and touched my shoulder saying, "Nikki, I just got the strangest feeling that it won't be long before I see Grannie again."

My mind would not even calculate what he was telling me. I brushed him away and said, "I don't even want to hear that, Dan."

Dan walked around the edge of the yard for a few minutes and quickly came back up to me once more. "Nikki, look at me. I have to tell you that I know it will not be long before I see her again."

My mouth fell open, and I abruptly recalled my dream. One week later, my brother Dan was hit by a car and thrown into an oncoming car left bleeding and dying on the highway. He had made his way to heaven. An old man lost control of his car and slid into Dan throwing him into the other lane of traffic. God had prepared me for what was about to come.

CHAPTER 24

DAN'S GONE

D AN'S ACCIDENT HAPPENED AROUND 9 PM that dreadful night in May. I was still extremely hurt over the loss of Grannie, as we all were. I sat down at the coffee table and began writing a poem called the *Road of Life*. Rarely had a poem or song flowed from me as freely as it did that night. I finished the poem and placed the pen down on the table. It was as if Dan were there telling me what to write. I had no way of knowing he was lying in the highway taking his last breath. I thought of the dream again and lay back on the couch staring at the ceiling just waiting. Anticipation filled the room. Why? What is this? What am I waiting for?

Suddenly, I heard a knock on the front door. I pulled the curtain back to find Colby, Jr. and Vern standing on the porch. Fear gripped me, and my first thought was Mama since Daddy was back in town. My bones were rattling as I unlocked the door. I knew this was the knock of death. Who? Where? What happened? I saw their faces and I began to tremble and cry.

"Nikki, it's Dan," Vern said. Vern grabbed one side and Junior grabbed the other, as I collapsed to the floor screaming in agony.

"He told me!" He told me! He told me!" I yelled. "I saw it in my dream! Dan told me in Grannie's yard."

Junior and Vern were pacifying a grieving sister and had no clue as to what I was referring to at the time.

"He gave me these words an hour ago. I wrote them down quickly and without thought," I said, as I held up the poem. "He told me!" I screamed again.

Elliot and Ella were awakened by my gut-wrenching screams. Poor little Ella was so frightened. I tried to regain my composure, but I just couldn't. "It's Dan," Vern said. "We've lost Dan."

Elliot helped me up off the floor and put me in the car with my brothers. "Go ahead and we will come later," he said.

I had to get to Mama. My precious Mama had lost her mother one week ago and now her son. As devastated as I was, it paled in comparison to her pain.

By the time we arrived to Mama's, the house was full of family. Mama was locked up in her bedroom racked with guilt and pain. "I should've kept him home with me," Mama groaned.

Mama was inconsolable. I had to get a grip on this, so I could be what I needed to be for her. My hands and feet had started going numb and drawing in. I thought I must be having a stroke from hyperventilating and all the crying. Carol gave me a paper sack to breathe deeply into. Slowly, I regained the feeling back in my limbs.

Hours later, Mama came out of the bedroom and sat down at the kitchen table. "I guess I need to try and get in contact with your Daddy," Mama said.

"Mama, I can do that for you," I said. "I saw him working one block from my house this week," I said.

Everyone stopped and listened, as I described the conversation we'd had. It was strange that we had not heard anything for four years, and now, during this time, he was here.

The poem was read at the funeral, and we sat in shock throughout the ceremony. Daddy came and sat in the back row. He was sober. He'd better be glad he was. He and Mama had a brief exchange of words, but that is all. We had lost Dan once to his illness and now to death.

CHAPTER 25
DADDY MOVES INTO MY MESS

THE EVENING OF DAN'S BURIAL, Ella and Elliot drove on home and left me checking on Mama. Carol gave me a ride home later that night, and when I got home, Ella was home alone. "Where is your brother?" I asked.

"He left about an hour ago," she said. "He told me he was going to the store and he would be back soon," said Ella.

I told Daddy after the funeral he could bring his camper and set it up behind the house if he needed to. He had his co-worker help him, and he was already set-up in the back yard by the time Carol and I arrived. His job would be leaving out of town in a few weeks, and I did want to see him. I was concerned about his loss of Dan, too. I wondered if it would make a difference in him somehow.

Ella went on to bed, and Carol and I were sitting up in the living room talking about everything. I started hearing Daddy ranting and raving in the back yard, throwing beer cans. Oh, what have I done? I can't take this! He's drunk! Carol went out and told him to try and have a little respect and go on to sleep.

"Naw, why ain't her husband here with her? "Where is that son of a b----?" Daddy yelled.

Ok, I appreciate you standing up for my honor, but this is ridiculous. Daddy finally calmed down and drifted off to sleep.

By this time, I was beginning to worry about Elliot. Where was he? He had left Ella here alone, and now I had a drunk father living behind the house. I was worried sick that something had happened to him. Carol stayed with me and tried to comfort me. Nightfall turned into day, and we were still awake, waiting for some kind of news about Elliot. I fixed Ella some breakfast and sent her off to school. Still no word on Elliot.

Carol and I got ready to go back to Mama's to check on her when I received a phone call from the county jail. It was a collect call from Elliot. It seems he decided it would be a great idea to leave Ella at home alone and go out to the club drinking the very night of my brother's burial. He had too much to drink, got a D.U.I., and got himself incarcerated.

"You can sit there and rot!" I screamed. I hung up that phone with every intention of leaving my husband in jail and moving on with life with Ella.

Daddy came up to the back door and heard me yelling. "What in the world is wrong with you, Nikki?" he asked.

"I have a husband in jail and that is where he is going to stay!" I exclaimed.

"Well, now, Nikki, you know I don't like him much, but you ought not to leave the ole boy in jail," Daddy said.

"Then YOU get him out, Daddy!" I hollered. "I just buried my Grannie and my brother! I don't have tolerance for such as this!" I shouted.

The weeks went by, and Daddy stayed drunk in the back yard. At least his age had slowed him down to some extent. He wasn't the same rowdy, old man as he had been during my childhood. Daddy finally moved out and left town with his job. He told me he would stay in touch with me through letters to let me know where he was. I really didn't care if he did or not. He was still drinking and I was sick of his advice on how to make my marriage work! Ha! Was he an expert?

I received the eviction notice, and this was the end of my marriage and almost the end of my sanity. Elliot did his time and got out, and I gave him no choice but to leave. I had saved my money and bought me a little Ford Pinto that was barely running. At least I didn't have to walk to work anymore and Ella had a way to school.

I told Elliot he could use my car to drive himself to the bus station, purchase a ticket, and leave. He packed his things and didn't even go in to tell Ella good-bye. He drove away on my little old car and kept on driving. Wow! I guess we really meant a lot to him, huh?

Ella and I would move into an apartment with a friend of mine from work until we could move out on our own. Hounded by bill collectors, garnishments on my wages for debt we'd collected together, I would surely have went under if it hadn't been for my singing job. I filed for bankruptcy and it would nearly be a year before I could save enough money for a divorce. Elliot would end up deceased under suspicious circumstances (suicide vs. homicide).

CHAPTER 26

ELLA LEAVES HOME

ELLA AND I WERE MAKING DO with next to nothing. She would walk to school, and I would walk to work. By this time, she was nearly sixteen-years-old. She was beginning to rebel, and I remember one afternoon I had to place her on restriction because of her talking back and disobeying my directions. I had to work, so there was really no way of properly enforcing the discipline once it was handed down to her. She was not allowed to use the phone. I unplugged the phone, and took it with me to work.

As my shift ended, I started home, and when I came around the corner near the ZipMart, I saw Ella standing there inside the pay phone booth, talking to her boyfriend. We lived in an era long before cell phones existed. I was livid! "Get your little behind back up to the house right now, young lady; you are on restriction!" I yelled. Ella slammed the phone receiver down and ran back to the house ahead of me.

I was supposed to go to the club that evening after work for band practice. How was I going to leave this girl on her own and enforce restriction? "I have to go to practice tonight and you're going with me," I said. "To the club?" she asked.

"Yes," I said. "Get your things."

The club would not be open to the public tonight, so I didn't have to worry about her being exposed to any drunk folks. We were just going for band practice, and I made her come with me just to prove my point. Looking back, I know it wasn't the brightest idea I ever had, but I had no choice. I had no one to watch her, and I needed to let her know how serious disobedience was and how she needed to adhere to the rules. I needed to listen to my own preaching. I was not obeying God, and I was out of the center of His will for my life.

She needed to know choices have consequences. She was miserable. I made her sit and listen to us sing while she was doing her homework at the table. I think it worked, at least for now. She had two more days of it, and I was going to try my best to make it hard on her. She was allowed to start using the phone again later that week. She hated me for days.

She was sixteen now. I had saved my money to buy her a new coat she wanted, so she wouldn't be cold walking to school. Things were going well. I was still singing on the weekends and working throughout the week. I suddenly realized I had not been asked to purchase any tampons in a while. When I got home from work, I called Ella into the living room and asked her to talk with me. "Are you alright?" I asked. "You haven't asked me to buy any personal items lately." I said.

Tears came streaming down her cheeks. "I'm pregnant," she said.

You could have blown me over with a feather. Ella was not the same sixteen-year-old that I was. She was giddy, immature, and clueless about the things of the world. I was sick. All I could do was hold her and rock her back and forth telling her "everything is going to be alright."

I blamed myself for not being available to her after school. How could I have done anything different? I had to work and pay the bills. I barely had enough to get us by. The credit fiasco Elliot left me with would take years to correct. I had to work each and every day.

Ella commenced to share with me that her boyfriend, Bob wanted to marry her and "do the right thing." I spoke with his parents, and they assured me he would be leaving for a career in the military as soon as he graduated in the summer, and he wanted Ella and his unborn child to be a part of his life.

The next few months Bob came to play a major role in Ella's life. He took her to each one of her doctor's visits and really proved to be a compassionate young man. Bob graduated in May, and he and Ella were wed in June on Ella's seventeenth birthday.

Bob left for boot camp training, and Ella followed soon afterwards to the military base where Bob was stationed. A healthy baby boy was born to Bob and Ella, and they were now parents. I hoped I had at least instilled some good in her. She settled comfortably into motherhood with a bright future ahead for her little family. I borrowed a band member's truck to make the trip to visit her new family. It was a special day that I will always be thankful for.

CHAPTER 27

A FRIENDSHIP BLOOMS IN THE DESERT

MY DAYS WERE LONELY NOW that Ella had moved out. This was the very first time in my life I had ever been completely alone. I was raised in a house full of siblings, had been married to Elliot, and then had Ella living with me. I was now completely alone. I felt as if I were walking in a dry wasteland as the sun parched my lips and torched my skin. There was no one in sight. One of my band members had been such a great friend to me through it all. His name was John. John had allowed me to use his truck many times when I needed to travel out of town.

I finally had enough money to go and consult with a lawyer. I was in dire need of bankruptcy and a divorce. As the consultation began, I spilled out the last few years of my life to this lawyer. "Put your money back in your pocket; this one is on the house," he said.

"I will pay you for your services, sir," I said.

"No ma'am, you most certainly will not," he said.

Within weeks, it was all over. I was divorced, and out from under the stress of garnishments. I was so thrilled to be free from that heavy load.

John began to drop by to see me from then on. I appreciated his help and friendship. Oh, that cupid really is a funny little fellow. Before I knew it, John and I were head over heels in love. Our friendship had sprung up out of the dry wasteland of my life and had bloomed into the most beautiful, life-giving, oasis I had ever known. We continued to play music together for the next four years, and we became the "talk of the town."

John proposed jokingly to me with a home-made bread-tie ring; I accepted. I still have that ring to this day. The deep, loving relationship John and I shared was no laughing matter. This was serious. Our wants, needs, and dreams ran parallel to one another. Our interests were one in the same. Our love of laughter and joy made my life the most peaceful I had ever known. He was the sweet peace I craved as a child. He was the absolute greatest friend I had ever known. This man was the man I would love and be loved by for the rest of my life. God had a plan.

We were married in the mountains one warm, August evening with Mama, Carol, and my cousin there to support me. When we came home, we held a reception in the yard with over two-hundred family members and friends. Daddy actually showed up, and he claimed he had quit drinking. What? That was hardly credible. I would have to investigate that to believe it.

Our love only deepened with each passing day. I began to feel the void of not having God at the center of this wonderful love. It had been years since I had spent time in prayer. I stayed under the constant conviction of the Holy Spirit.

John had gone to bed, and I knelt down in the living room and quietly whispered, "Father, please forgive me for not talking to you as I should have. Please forgive me of my countless sins and come and make a way back in our lives." I knew that having God at the center of this relationship would be like icing on the cake.

John had to work the next morning, and his office was at the top of two flights of stairs. He made his way to the office and sat down to have his first cup of coffee. His fingers began to tingle, and he sat the cup down on the table. Immediately after, his hand, and then his arm started feeling funny. He made his way down the two flights of stairs and drove himself to the hospital.

John waited until 3 PM before he had his brother call me to let me know he was at the hospital. I was working for a full-line vending company at the time stocking drink machines and snack machines in large industrial businesses. When I got that call, my heart began to ache, tears began to flow, and I did nothing but pray all the way to the hospital. A co-worker drove me into town because I was too upset to drive safely.

When I arrived at the emergency room, John's son, William met me outside. "What am I about to walk into?" I asked through my tears.

"Nikki, he's stable, but he has been very sick since they gave him the dye for the CAT scan," William said. "He's completely paralyzed on the right side of his body, but he can talk to you and communicate well," William said.

I rushed in and found John's room. He was lying back in the bed, and I grabbed him and held him in my arms for a moment. "I love you," I said. "I'm here, and I will not leave here without you," I said.

John held me close, and we both began to cry. He was scared, and so was I, but we knew no matter what, we would get through this together.

CHAPTER 28

TRADEGY BRINGS TRIUMPH

THE FIRST DAY IN THE HOSPITAL with John will forever be etched in my memories. I knelt down at an altar of prayer and asked God to protect his life. I promised God if He would protect him and heal him, I would completely abandon my old life and live for Him. I re-dedicated my life back to God right there in that room.

The road would be tough, but John was determined to get better. His diagnosis was spinal stenosis of the neck region. His spinal column basically closed in on the spinal cord and paralyzed his right side from his neck to his toes. He was incapacitated, and physical therapy had to be ordered for him to recover. He was in a wheelchair for months and could not stand on his own without assistance. He couldn't even sit up on the edge of the bed without losing his balance and falling over. He was broken and angry.

The doctors recommended that John stay in a rehabilitation program in the hospital for many weeks, but I brought him home. I took him to outpatient therapy treatments each week and watched as the therapists assisted him in regaining his functional abilities through exercise and therapeutic activities. I wanted to learn all that I could to help him. A friend of ours, Mike, came out and added handrails on the inside all the way down the hallway, so we could practice walking when John was able. I bet he walked a thousand miles back and forth holding onto those handrails.

By October of that year, John had regained his functional ability in his leg and could stand and walk on his own. He had a brace in his shoe that prevented his right foot from dragging and tripping him when he walked. He walked with a significant limp, but he was walking, and we were so thankful for that. He still had great deficits in his hand and finger function, but he was now able to perform his activities of daily living with little or no assistance from me. He decided to go back to work. I remember saying a prayer over him that morning.

I knew it would be hard on him emotionally to return to the office and have his peers watching him walk for the first time after the event. He pulled up in the parking lot and shut off the truck. Climbing down out of the truck, he said he saw what seemed like a hundred co-workers standing on the porch of his office. He had to cross the street and walk into the door where each one of those workers was standing. His gait looked like a person's gait when they are trying to recover from a stroke. He swallowed his pride and got out, limping all the way.

Not one single person cracked a joke or laughed at him. Instead, he got multiple handshakes, hugs, and cheers. John was a very well-respected man, and he treated his employees with great respect as well. Everyone loved him, which was obvious to me while we were in the hospital! Our lives completely changed the moment he was paralyzed. I knew God was up to something, but I could not see what it was just yet. I know it instantly humbled my husband and caused me to turn back to the Lord.

As John sat down on his first day back at the office, he received a phone call. His sister, Deana, called screaming to the top of her lungs. "John," she screamed, "Oh my God; Robert has been shot!"

"Where is he; in the hospital?" John asked.

"Listen, Robert just shot himself in the head, and he is dead; he didn't make it," said Deana.

John immediately hung up the phone and told his co-workers he had to go. John called me with the news. I could not imagine the pain he was feeling. The emotional ride he was on was just too much. We were numb. We were angry! We wanted answers. This just could not real, but it was. His older brother, Robert had committed suicide.

The next few months of healing mentally and physically were even harder now for John. I just kept on loving him, and I prayed his heart would soften, and it seemed the more I prayed, the angrier he became. He continued his therapy at home and continued to work. He tried to stay busy and keep his mind off of everything.

One day, out of the clear blue, he asked me if I'd like to go to church. I tried to contain my excitement, but inside I was about to explode. He surrendered his life back to Christ, and God began to build a ministry out of the ashes of our lives. We never set foot in a nightclub again after his paralysis.

CHAPTER 29
A PROMISE KEPT

I T WAS THE HOTTEST SUMMER ON RECORD that year in
our South Alabama town. I knew it more than most, as I had tak-
en a job with the local dry cleaner as a presser. The equipment in
that place should have been outlawed. I had never seen anything
quite like it. The foot pedals closed the large, cast iron plate down
on the clothing, and then you'd have to hit the button with your
hand to shoot the steam to it. The steam would go right in the middle of your face each time it closed. There was no air-conditioning
in that "sweat shop," and only one industrial fan that blew nothing
but hot air. I was working hard, as I always did.

I left the full-line vending company after John's paralysis, with
plans to possibly go to college one day for physical therapy, so that
I could continue to help him heal. John kept encouraging me to
go get my G.E.D. I was so afraid I would not pass it and have to
suffer that embarrassment. I had no self-confidence, but John saw
something in me that I had not seen in myself.

"You are so intelligent," John said. "I know you'll pass if you just
go take the test."

My self-esteem was at an all-time low, but John did not give up encouraging me. "Here's the money; now go take the test," he insisted.

"I'm going to be so humiliated when I come back home, and you are going to be out this money!" I exclaimed.

I had been out of high school for fifteen years. I was certain I would fail, and that I needed to study first. John dropped me off at the learning center where the test was given that day, and I did not come back out until I completed the test.

I went on back to work pressing clothes and forgot about the G.E.D. Back then, you had to wait for your results to come in the mail. Oh, well, back to reality. I was not thrilled about going to the cleaners, but I was thankful for a job. Hard work hadn't killed me yet. If roofing didn't kill me, this surely won't. If you can roof a house and hang with the likes of Colby Winslow, you can do anything.

Weeks went by, and I went on working at the cleaners. The days kept getting hotter. I would go home to do laundry and have salt deposits on my clothing. I was busy working one day, and I heard the familiar voice of John as he walked into the back door of the cleaners.

"Hey, Baby!" He pulled a package out from behind his back and said, "I thought you'd like to see this surprise I have for you," he said.

It was a brown envelope, and as I opened it, I kept looking to John for some kind of clue. It was my G.E.D. I had passed with flying colors on the very first try without having to study for it! It was just like John told me it would be. I screamed so loud and grabbed him and jumped into his arms.

"You did it, Nikki!" he said. "You are extremely intelligent and don't let anyone ever tell you that you're not," said John.

I dropped out of school years ago. I must be dreaming. Did that just happen? I carefully read the document and inspected it to make sure it was real and not some cruel joke. My name was spelled correctly, and as I looked at the date it was issued, I began to cry. It was issued on Mama's birthday. I had finally kept my promise to her, and she would receive a neatly packaged copy of this document for her birthday that year.

"Happy Birthday, Mama," I whispered through my tears of joy.

CHAPTER 30
A MEMORABLE MEMORIAL DAY

WHAT AN IMPOSSIBLE DREAM! I had the kindest, most encouraging husband a woman could ever hope for. We decided I would start college in January and start the year off fresh. I had core classes that I had to get through before I could even begin to think about physical therapy classes. I would work during the day and attend classes at night until I got finished with core classes.

I started a new job at the local hospital as a medical transcriptionist, and I had never taken a typing class in my life. The favor of God was on me. Now, I could slowly work into all of the skills I would need to be successful in my pursuit of this dream. Medical terminology and typing would definitely be part of college life for me. I needed practice and lots of it. I learned very quickly and became one of fastest typist on the job.

I left work one day and headed for the store to pick up a few items. It was Memorial Day weekend, and we had a family reunion planned in a few weeks. I stopped by to pick up cleaning supplies, and while I was in the store, I experienced the greatest pain my body I had ever known. I had the deepest, excruciating pain in my right side just under my rib cage. It stopped me in the aisle and lasted briefly. I went on down the aisle, and it hit again. This time it hit so hard that I fell over the buggy in pain. A woman in the store helped me out to the car and asked if she could drive me back to the hospital. The pain eased off in the midst of my prayers, and I thanked the lady and drove on to the E.R.

Why would it come and go so suddenly? I didn't know what was going on, but I knew something was definitely wrong. I have a high tolerance for pain, but this was off the charts. I called John and Mama to let them know where I was.

Two days before I landed in the E.R. I had gone horseback riding with my uncle. The horse was frightened by a rabbit and suddenly jumped in the ditch causing me to lose my grip, and go flying out onto the dirt road face first. It knocked the breath out of me and took me a minute to regain my air. I remember my right side hurting a little, but I climbed back on and kept riding. I wondered if maybe this pain was caused by that accident earlier in the week. But why would it be delayed?

The doctor decided to send me for CAT scan of the abdomen, and after the tests, he discovered what appeared to be a large cyst on my right ovary. We scheduled the surgery to remove the cyst for the next morning. I had not been admitted in the hospital for anything since I was born. I almost didn't make it to the hospital then. Mama says I was nearly born on the back of Daddy's motorcycle on the way to the hospital. Ha! Born to be different, I guess. Ha!

We were all shocked and dismayed to discover the real reason for my pain. The tests the doctor ran prior to the surgery did not show what was really there. All they were able to visualize was the ovary. When I regained consciousness after the operation, John and Mama were in the room with me. I asked John, "Well, am I gonna live?"

John looked at me and smiled, and gently and began to tell this unbelievable tale of what happened. "Nikki, this may come as quite a shock to you, but I need to tell you what this was," said John. "The doctor diagnosed you with having a teratoma, which is a benign tumor that was supposed to have been your very own twin/sibling," said John. "It had hair, teeth, and blood vessels with its own blood supply," John stated.

Now, John was famous for making me laugh uncontrollably, so I waited to see him burst out into erroneous laughter. John never smiled, and I could tell by the way Mama was looking that he was telling me the truth.

I didn't realize the extent of the emotional effects of this operation until we returned home. I began to battle with depression and even some separation anxiety. How could I feel like this about a tumor? It was supposed to have been my twin? Wait…what? Why was I having these feelings of loss? Mama was having them, too. She came over to check on me, and we talked in depth about everything.

"Nikki, I've never told anyone about this, but when I was pregnant with you, I felt like I was carrying twins; I had even picked out two names," Mama said. "You always did try to carry the load for others, didn't you?" Mama asked.

Mama and I cried for awhile and held onto each other. God had spared my life and allowed me to live another day. I was so thankful, and my faith just drew stronger as time went by.

Our singing had become a traveling music ministry, and we were going forth sharing our testimonies with every crowd we encountered. God had worked miracles in our lives, and we knew who we were singing for. The music had purpose, and we could feel it.

CHAPTER 31

BECOMING A THERAPIST

J ANUARY CAME AND IT WAS TIME to enroll in college. It was such a different and more satisfying experience compared to high school. Nobody knew me or where I came from. Nobody knew I was a high school dropout or the poorest child in the county. It was an equal playing field. I excelled in all of my core classes, and I had a 4.0 grade-point average. Me? On the Presidents list? Dean's list? Maybe I am pretty smart. Who knew? I was determined to get accepted into the therapy program. I wrote my essay, all core classes had been done, I achieved all of my volunteer hours required, and my grades were perfect. I was set to send in my application.

College was about to start for the Summer semester the next day, and during the night we got a phone call that John's sister, Rita, had suddenly passed away with a heart attack. I was so thankful I had not turned in my application for the program yet. I needed to be there for John again, and nothing was going to stop me from that. John had suffered a great deal of heartache the last few years. My heart hurt for him.

I went on to apply for the next class of students, and I was accepted on the first try. I got called in for an interview! I got in! Now, I was on my way to making this dream a reality. It was a very challenging program, but with lots of encouragement from John, and many, many prayers, I was able to push through to become a therapist. I was even elected class President, and graduated with honors in the top three of my class. "Me?" I have to ask. Even as I'm writing this now it doesn't seem real. No one from high school would believe this.

I had just found my first therapy job and started working when John's mother passed away. It seemed for everything good we had three more bad things that happened, but we pressed on. We knew what loss was. We knew what pain was, and we channeled that all into our music ministry through songwriting.

CHAPTER 32
ANGELS DO EXIST

MANY SOULS HAD COME TO KNOW THE LORD through the work John and I were doing for Kingdom of God. We were able to share the tremendous testimonies to countless people. God had blessed us both so much through every trial, giving us strength to stand and declare the wonderful works of the Lord. My walk with Jesus was closer now than it had ever been.

Several years went by, and the ministry began to grow. God had opened the floodgates of heaven and rained down upon us. We were so thankful. Our music began to be recognized, not only on a national level, but we also became cast members on three different global television network shows, which reached literally millions of people. We still lived down a dirt road, and we wouldn't have it any other way. If we were anything to anybody, it was ONLY because of God, and we made that clear. He alone was worthy of praise. It was ALL for Him and His kingdom work, and it still is. God took a little girl, who came from nothing by worldly standards, and placed her in front of the worldwide audience, reaching millions of souls for the Kingdom of God through a song.

We drifted off to sleep one evening at home, and around 2 AM, I was awakened by the worst pain I'd ever had. I felt as if I were having a heart attack. The pain was unbearable under my breast bone (sternum). I sat straight up in bed, and began to pray what I thought must be my last prayer on earth. I prayed for God to please give me more time. I was so exhausted and had just got out of the hospital from having my gallbladder removed several weeks prior to this incident. "Lord, just please give me some more time," I prayed.

Just as soon as I finished those words, I felt the sensation of being lifted up out of the bed and heard the sound of all the air being sucked up out of the room. I was floating above the bed, looking down at where me and John were lying. I could see us lying there asleep. I looked over my right shoulder and then my left shoulder. Behind each shoulder was a big, beautiful, white wing that reached to the ceiling. I began to praise God, and then I heard the sound of the air being drawn back into the room and the sensation of being lowered back down to my body in bed. The pain was completely gone from my body.

I had an experience with the Lord that day, and no one can convince me otherwise. I had supernatural healing in my body. I was wide awake, and I began to shout and praise God so loud that I woke John up. "What is going on?" John asked.

"I was healed from something just now," I said. It would be years before I experienced any more physical pain.

CHAPTER 33
DADDY'S SOBRIETY

YEARS DRIFTED BY SINCE I HAD LAST SEEN DADDY. Last I heard, he was sober. Ha! I found that amusing to say the least. I was unaware that my childhood prayer had come true. John encouraged me to find him and visit him since he was getting older, and he was my Daddy. John really didn't understand our history. I have always loved my Daddy in spite of all of the trauma he subjected us to growing up. I was now an adult, and the past was past. I tried to take John's advice and reach out to him.

I found him down in Florida. He was alone and had recently been placed on disability. He worked extremely hard all of his life, and his joints in his legs finally gave out. He was crawling on his hands and knees still trying to lay carpet up until his disability kicked in. He could barely walk, and John found it hard to believe this man was the one I had described.

"He seems like such a jolly ole fellow," said John.

"Yeah!" I said sarcastically. "You just don't know!"

My emotions were bouncing around in fifty different directions. I had compassion on this elderly man, but I did remember what he had done so many years before. The terror and fear he caused was still fresh in my memory even though it had been years since I had tasted any of it.

John and I began visiting with Daddy from time to time. I wanted to sneak down there unannounced and catch him drinking. If I could do that, then this new "relationship" or whatever you call it could end before it started. I still wanted to be mad at him.

Each time we'd go down to see him, John would once again remind me of what a "nice fellow" he is. "He's so much fun to be around," John said.

"I still don't trust him," I said. "I'll bet he is popping the lid off one right now," I said. This suspicion went on for years. Daddy had claimed to be sober now for 15 years. I let my guard down. I finally believed him and took him at his word.

Our visits got more frequent, and he even came to spend a night or two along with us. I never mentioned our past, even though Daddy would sometimes try to apologize. I would cut him off in the middle of his sentence and change the subject. I did not want to discuss the matter with him at all. My coping mechanism for decades was to just shove it down so far and forget about it.

Sometimes he would say things like, "I never hit your Mama but one time"...Are you kidding me? I was there, and I lived every awful night of his evil behavior. Did he really think in his mind that I could have forgotten any of it? Did he really convince himself that he only hit her ONE time? Come on, what kind of an idiot did he think I was?

I know he was in the early stages of Alzheimer's dementia, but I was infuriated by comments like that. So, it was best that Daddy and I never discuss our past at all. I would just pretend that I had forgiven him, and he could pretend it never happened. That is how we tolerated one another.

CHAPTER 34

GOD PREPARES ME FOR FORGIVENESS

MY HEART BECAME TENDER for Daddy as he began to age and have trouble walking. I tried to help him anyway I could with John's encouragement.

In October, we were singing in a small church in Georgia and the Holy Spirit spoke directly to me saying, "Do not fear for you are my flower, and I have chosen you to reveal great things through you."

Again in October of the same year, miles away in another church in Alabama, the Holy Spirit spoke directly to me saying, "Do not fear, my daughter; I do not make mistakes. My plans will be revealed in you."

Ok, I'm beginning to see a pattern here. What's next, Lord? One week later in a church miles away from the last one the Holy Spirit spoke directly to me again saying, "Do not be afraid, my daughter; I created you to work for me."

What was going to happen? I knew God had used dreams and prophecy before to prepare me for what was about to happen. I just prayed and prayed for guidance and protection. In November, Carol called me. I had not mentioned any of the messages I had received one month prior. Carol said, "I just had to call you because Denny, (Carol's youngest son), has something he wants to tell you."

Denny was only three-years-old. He got on the phone with me and began to quote this scripture, "Let not your heart be troubled"....I do believe I have had a word from Almighty God not to fear what was about to take place in my life and to trust Him.

CHAPTER 35
MERRY CHRISTMAS; HERE IT IS

O CTOBER THROUGH NOVEMBER God was preparing me for something. I was about to find out just what it was with one quick trip to see Daddy.

John and I drove down on December 11th to visit him in Florida and take him his Christmas present. He had a visitor that day who I had never met before. He was a middle-aged man named Rick. Daddy said he was a neighbor that helped him fix things around the house. As I stood up to shake Rick's hand and introduce myself, the hair on the back of my neck stood on end.

We had a nice visit with Daddy, and I gave him a hug good-bye. As soon as the car door slammed, and we drove out of his yard, I immediately told John, "The Holy Spirit is telling me that something is not right down here." John and I discussed it all the way home. I prayed for Daddy's safety, and I called and checked on him after we got back home.

Several days passed by, and Christmas came and went. It was now December 26th, and I called a friend of mine to discuss my

155

concerns about my aging father and his health. I spoke about how I was praying for a way for him to move closer by so that I might be able to offer my help as he continued to age. Another friend called to share with us about how our music had touched the heart and soul of a drug addict, and she was going to go to church on Sunday.

As we hung up the phone with that friend, John and I began praising the Lord for that wonderful news! In the middle of our praise, the phone rang again. I answered the call and it was Daddy's landlord. Oh no! Why would she be calling? Was Daddy dead? I often feared he would be found dead and alone. Even as bad as he was to us growing up, I didn't want him to die alone and unsaved.

"Nikki, this is Mrs. Barrett, and I need to let you know...you're Daddy," she said... "He's"...

I was so sure she was going to tell me he was dead. I slid down onto the floor and braced myself for what was about to come. "He's...been arrested for drug trafficking!"

WHAT!

"You will need to come and remove all of his things from his home because he's in jail," she said.

"Thank you for calling, Mrs. Barrett," I said. "I will get down there just as quick as I can to start on that."

My 72-year-old father on oxygen was busted for drug trafficking for selling his prescription pain medications to an undercover officer. He was facing 10 years in prison and a $50,000 bond. He would spend the rest of his short life in jail, as far as I could see.

All of his children put together could not afford to bond him out, and none of us had any assets free and clear. We all owed money on everything we were working for. No land or other items that we could put up as collateral. What a mess!

I spent the next few days crying, shouting, hurting, screaming, and praying. Why was this all of sudden my problem? Why was I the one that was supposed to move his things out and check on him in jail? He had other children, too.

I stretched out on the floor and buried my face in my arms crying. "So, this is it, huh, Lord?" I asked. "I am the one to take care of his mess. How, Lord?" I asked. "How?"

A sweet peace lingered over the room, and my crying stopped as I continued to lay face down in the floor. "Get up and give me all that you have," the Holy Spirit said.

I made my way to my knees and lifted my hands in praise. "Thank you, Lord, for this trial that will bring you glory! Thank you, Lord; I praise you Lord."

A gentle calm swept over me, and I knew what I had to do. I would be the one to bring Daddy back. My childhood prayers for his salvation would come to pass if only I obeyed the guidance of the Holy Spirit. Somehow, I knew God would be glorified through this mess. My flesh did not want this task, but I knew God had hand-picked me for it. My spirit was willing to be led into whatever path God needed me to walk. In the midst of the unsurmountable emotions, I found the strength to praise Him.

CHAPTER 36
THE MOVE

I CALLED THE JAIL MANY TIMES throughout the next few weeks checking on Daddy. He was on oxygen, and they had brought a wheelchair to him because he could barely get around. I spoke to a jailer who reassured me that Daddy was not in the general population, but in medical lockdown. He was being monitored by the nursing staff.

I took an unscheduled vacation from work and drove down to begin packing up Daddy's things and to take care of his bills. I loaded, packed, cleaned, and straightened day in and day out. He had multiple loaded guns scattered in and under things throughout the house. I found a pistol in a canister, one under the couch cushion, and even one wrapped in a towel and neatly placed in a bucket in the closet. Daddy had a total of seven guns that I found when packing, all loaded and ready to use. I also found knives of all shapes and sizes, a machete, a baseball bat, and a set of brass knuckles. He was ready for anything. Wow! I sure didn't have to worry about him taking care of himself living alone. A burglar wouldn't stand a chance if they broke in on this old man! He was still mighty strong to be an elderly man, but I guess having the weapons gave him more confidence to defend himself as he grew older.

The drive down to Florida took approximately 2 and ½ hours one way, so I spent countless hours that week trying to get the move completed. I rented a storage shed in town to store his things. I was exhausted from going back and forth. One more trip down and back should have it. I was so thankful I was nearing the end of this duty.

During the early morning hours, I received a phone call from Ella. "Good morning!" she said.

"Ella, hey there; how are you doing, sweetie?" I asked.

"I just wanted to call and check on you," she said.

"I'm alright, but I still haven't finished moving all of Daddy's things!" I said.

Ella was remarried to a new fellow, and she had four children at this point in time. "Well, I can use Kevin's work van and meet you there at lunch to help you finish the last load," she offered.

"That would be wonderful!" I cried. "I could use all the help I can get."

I got ready and drove on down to Florida to meet Ella at the steakhouse for lunch. We had a nice conversation over a warm meal and had fun catching up on her new life and new husband, Kevin. She was doing great, and I was so proud of what a great mother she'd become. We finished lunch, and she followed me on out to Daddy's place.

"I've just got this one last load and I will be finished!" I said excitedly. "This has been a huge undertaking," I said.

As we packed the last box on my truck and filled Kevin's work van with furniture, I went back to lock the front door and turn in Daddy's key. I was finished! This would be the last time I would have to come down here for a while. We headed out for the storage shed in South Alabama with Ella driving Kevin's van and me driving my truck behind her. Whew! I was so thankful to be done with that hectic job! This is the very last load!

I am driving a truck with a seat full of guns and various other weapons and boxes, and Ella has the contents of Daddy's medicine cabinets and the last of the furniture with her. Just as we make it across the state line of Florida and head into Alabama, Ella swerves on the van and is stopped by a State Trooper.

I pulled off the shoulder of the road behind them. The trooper got out, and I recognized him from high school. It was Chuck Wall. "Hi, Chuck," I said. "It's Nikki Winslow (Brannon) from school.

"Hey, Nikki, are y'all traveling together?" he asked.

"Yes, this is my sister-in-law, and she's helping me move Daddy's things to the storage shed," I stated.

Ella got out of the van and told the officer, "The reason I swerved was because I dropped my hamburger in my lap."

Chuck had a canine partner named Kilo. The dog was barking and going to the front of the van. "Nikki, please step back and wait over there for me," said Chuck. "My dog has just alerted on this vehicle."

Oh, my Lord! What in the name of all goodness? Ella? No, she couldn't have anything in her husband's van that would cause this situation to get any worse. Could she? I immediately thought of the arsenal of weapons I had just hauled across the state line and the medicines that must be in any number of those boxes we had just packed up for Daddy. Oh dear God! What if he searches my truck, too? I began to pray and ask for the protection of God on my life. Chuck asked for permission to search the van Ella was driving.

"It's my husband's work van, and I have no idea what you might find in here," Ella said.

I spoke up and told Chuck that everything in the very back of the van belonged to my father, and she was not responsible for it. "She's been helping for nearly 10 hours today," I said.

The search was on. The dog kept alerting to the dash of the van. Lord, please! What on earth is that dog finding? We are totally innocent of any wrongdoing, but what if he wants to search my truck? I KNOW I have enough weapons in that truck to send me to jail right now! I just traveled across the state lines with weapons of all sorts and now...an alerting canine officer?

I focused on Chuck, and he started walking towards me. Oh my God! I'm about to have a heart attack. I'm sweating profusely, and I haven't done anything but try and move an elderly man's belongings back to Alabama and put them in a storage shelter until he gets out of prison.

"Nikki, we are going to have to lock her up," Chuck said.

"What did you find?" I asked.

"We found a crack pipe on the dash hidden underneath a pile of mail," he said.

"I promise it's not mine!" Ella screamed. "This van belongs to my husband and he uses it for work! It's not mine!" she yelled.

The handcuffs were placed around Ella's wrist, and they led her to the patrol car.

"Nikki, you sure didn't need this interference!" she cried. "I swear I'm telling the truth!" she stated.

"Ella, I believe you, honey but what a mess!" I sighed.

Chuck placed Ella in the back of the patrol car and came back over to me saying, "Call someone to help you take the van to unload your Daddy's things. She's going to jail tonight for drug paraphernalia," said Chuck.

I stood in amazement that I was going to be able to get the LAST load unpacked, and my truck was not searched. My God had His hand on my life, freedom, career, and ministry that night. If any other officer had stopped Ella that night, my world would've changed forever. God shot down Satan's plans to destroy me and get me through this trial.

I unloaded the last box and crammed it into the unit. The door got stuck on the box and I just kicked it on in and locked it up tightly. I was furious! All of this unnecessary headache almost cost me MY life as well. I was so mad at Daddy for putting me in this predicament. I was so mad at Ella and her husband. I was mad at my siblings for not coming to help me sufficiently. I was mad!

I made it home and finally got into bed. John grabbed me, and hugged me, as I shared the episode of the night with him. I tried to relax and drift off to sleep. I tossed and turned for hours. "Go on and get her out, Nikki," John whispered. "I know you will not rest until you do," he said.

Ella had four children waiting for her at home. She was trying to help me, and her husband's habit nearly destroyed both our lives. It could have just as easily been me in the cell with her if the trooper had searched my truck.

I got dressed and bonded her out. She was so happy and surprised to see me. "Come on and spend the night with me tonight," I said. "You get home to those babies in the morning," I said.

"I will make this right, Nikki," she said.

We drove to my house and I went onto bed. What a night to remember!

CHAPTER 37

UNEXPECTED OUTCOME

I T WAS NOW FEBRUARY, and Daddy had been in jail since the day after Christmas. I called each chance I got to check on him. His court date was coming up on the 15th, and I was much in prayer about his situation. I just didn't see a way out for him, and we couldn't afford to bond him out. He would have to sit there for the remainder of his life unless things changed.

John and I drove down on his court date to have the chance to see him and offer him some moral support. When they called Daddy's name to enter the court room, the jailer wheeled him into the place in a wheelchair. He looked terrible. I began to cry. I was incredibly angry with him, and I harbored a significant amount of animosity towards him, but when they brought him in before me, I broke down. God filled my heart with compassion. I saw my aging father in tremendous need of encouragement and support. I started to pray the judge would have mercy on him and lighten his sentence.

The judge looked at John and me and asked, "Are you related to this man?"

"Yes, your Honor; this is my father." I said.

The charges were read against Daddy, and the judge began to hand down his decision on bond hearing. "I am going to reduce this bond from $50,000 down to $5,000, which means this man can get out and go home with his family for $500 today," said the Judge.

John and I were speechless, and our world was about to change. What? Nobody gets off this easy in the state of Florida on these charges! What just happened? Did they release my father to my custody? "John, what does this mean?" I asked.

"It means we are going to have an instant house guest," said John.

Wow! I was NOT ready for that. He was now homeless, and the judge released him in my care. I was responsible for him now. If he jumped bond, I would have to pay the bondsmen the bill. Was I the one now responsible for keeping him in line? That was obviously impossible. Now, he would be in my house! He would be under my roof! I began to cry harder as reality set in. I didn't want him to live with me! I was angry and bitter at everything he had caused me to deal with lately; not to mention the past.

The ride home was not much fun. The more he talked, the more intense my anger became.

"I didn't do what they say I did, darlin'," Daddy said.

"I'm in no mood to talk about it right now," I said. "You have no idea what all of this has done to me!" I screamed. "Just hush and thank God you are a free man," I said.

Love, hate, love, hate. I was confused. Let the "fun" begin!

CHAPTER 38

IT'S RAINING

THE DAYS AT OUR HOME were filled with mixed emotions. John thought Daddy was the most interesting old fellow. He laughed at his jokes and talked with him for hours. I was not happy about that, either. Yeah, it's all fun and games now, huh? I wanted Daddy to feel what I had been feeling since December. The stress of the move, the feeling of being alone in this trial, and the agony of knowing you couldn't do anything but wait and pray. He was happy. I was not! The turmoil was eating me alive, and now I had him in the house with me each and every day. Help me, Lord! Why? I know I'm not supposed to ask why but...why? His dementia had worsened, and he repeated the same story over and over some days. I just wanted him to shut up! My patience was growing mighty thin.

The next month in March, John and I had a granddaughter born premature at 23 weeks. Her name was Layla. We rushed to the hospital, and I held her in the palm of my right hand. She was so tiny and frail. I prayed over that child. She was in my arms, and I was rocking her in the chair in the hospital room when she took her last breath. I was beyond help. My spirit ripped from within me. I laid her down in the bed just as she passed, and I noticed the white blanket behind her was folded in the shape of two angel wings. I took a picture of her on my new cell phone, kissed her tiny little head and we prepared for a funeral.

I got home and there he was. Daddy was sitting in my recliner. I was disgusted! I didn't want to see his face. He didn't have any idea what I was going through. I went into the bedroom and slammed my door.

"John, what happened?" Daddy asked.

"Mr. Colby, we lost our little granddaughter just now," he said.

"Oh," said Daddy.

Oh? Is that all he can say to that comment? Whew, I was mad! I just wanted to throw him out right then and there. How could he know how I'm feeling? I began to cry and pray. I was once again face down on the bedroom floor. I had spent a lot of time on my face before the Lord since December. It was going to take a lot of Jesus to get through these days. I was gently reminded as I prayed that Daddy really did know what I was feeling. He and Mama had lost little Ray years ago and Dan, also.

I stayed locked up in that room for days as we planned the funeral. We ordered a tiny little casket, bought a tiny blanket of flowers, and I went shopping for a pink dress for her to wear to meet Jesus. I remember while in the store I could not find a dress small enough to fit her. I saw a tiny baby doll in the window and asked the sales lady to take it down for me. The dress would be a perfect fit.

The Lord began to pour out His strength upon us through song during this time. We were writing a song a week for weeks as we fought to keep our sanity.

CHAPTER 39
FULL CIRCLE

MONTHS WENT BY, AND I STRUGGLED with my relationship with Daddy. I just could not take any more. Regardless of my responsibility of signing his bond, I was done! I needed him out of my house. I was losing my mind. I couldn't grieve the loss of Layla the way I needed to for arguing with him about trying to keep him out of jail. He was on probation and under strict rules. He was not supposed to have a gun or leave the state. I was tired of arguing with him about why he should abide by the rules. If he wanted to risk going to prison and dying there, I was all too obliging to allow him to do what he wanted.

I found him a small house about five miles away from me. I rented the house for him, and he could have every gun he had and take it with him. "If you get caught, do NOT call me to help!" I demanded.

We got him moved out and at last, I had the chance to fall apart. I crumbled. I stayed in the floor for days, up and down. I was relieved, yet anticipating when Daddy would get caught and die in prison. After all of the mess he had just come through and got out of, he was willing to risk it all to have his guns. I was sick! I had to release every part of this to God, or I would die.

My prayer life became deeply intense. I knew what I had to do. I needed to forgive. Forgive? Daddy? I had forgiven Daddy years ago for what he had done. Or did I? Is this why you placed him in my home, Lord? Are you trying to reveal this to me? I was sure I had forgiven him long ago. I was so wrong.

Daddy had been out of the house for three months, and I had not been to see him or talked to him on the phone since he left. I had John stopping by to check on him. Everything was fine, and I just needed a complete break from all of it. I didn't think that was too much to ask after all I had experienced since December. I told John to just tell him I needed some time to recover from all of it. Daddy told him he understood. I doubted that he really knew, but whatever.

One afternoon, I got a call phone from my brother Ron. "Nikki, Daddy is very sick, and I wanted to see if you could come check on him," he said.

Oh, here we go. "I guess I can," I said. "Lord, you've got to help me get right about this," I said. "I can't do this on my own!"

John and I drove over, and when we got there, Daddy was sitting in his recliner pale as a ghost. He had beads of sweat popping off his forehead, and I knew he needed medical attention. I checked his blood pressure, and it was extremely high. He must be having a heart attack. He was talking to me in a high pitched voice.

"Come on and let's take you to the hospital, Daddy," I said.

"No, I'm not going tonight!"

"Well, at least let me call an ambulance," I said.

"No, I'll be fine tonight, but you can take me to the doctor in the morning," Daddy said.

I had exhausted all of my vacation time with everything since December, and I had to rely on John to take him. John picked Daddy up and took him into the doctor's office that morning. They admitted him into the hospital for tests. I would go by each morning before work, on my lunch break, and after work every day to check on Daddy. He was much weaker and short of breath. He could barely stand on his feet, so I'd help him back and forth to the bedside commode.

"Darlin', I never would have thought that one of young'uns would have to wipe my behind. I'm so sorry," Daddy said.

"If I can do this for a complete stranger at work, I should be able to do this for my own father, Daddy. Don't worry about it," I said.

God broke me down during the days of his hospitalization. I knew I was being tested and even prepared for this. I surely didn't know the outcome of this, but I was humbled and willing to do what God needed, and (what Daddy needed) me to do. He stayed in the local hospital for five days as test results started to come in. He had been diagnosed with atrial fibrillation and coronary artery disease with chronic obstructive pulmonary disease. His blood pressure dropped very low, and I became very concerned. I still didn't want to believe he was in that much danger yet.

I called my siblings and informed them that Daddy was sick, and he had been in the hospital for days. Each one of them came by to see

Daddy and had a good visit with him. Fences were mended that day. Daddy looked at John and asked, "Reckon what it feels like to die?"

I told Daddy, "I guess it would be alright if a person was ready to meet Jesus." Daddy smiled.

I went by to see him that morning before work, and I told him I would stop back by at lunch just as I had been doing. Carol came down and sat with Daddy that day. About an hour before lunch, Carol called me to tell me that Daddy was being transferred to a larger hospital to see a cardiologist. I told Carol I would be over there as soon as I got off work.

I clocked out that day and called John to let him know Daddy had been transferred. John said, "I don't know why, but something told me to meet you in town."

I met John at the local grocery store and parked my car. We drove over to visit Daddy. When we arrived, my brother Ron and sister Carol were in the room with him. Carol said, "I'm so glad you made it because he's been asking for you all day long!" she said.

Carol and Ron left the room with John. Daddy said, "I think I need to scoot up more in the bed so I can breathe better."

I assisted Daddy further up towards the head of the bed, and he grabbed my hand. "I love you, Daddy," I said.

Daddy squeezed my hand and said, "Darlin', I love you, too."

At the precise moment we shared those sincere words with one another, Daddy turned his head and had a massive heart attack right in front of me. "Nurse! "Nurse!"

I began to perform a sternal rub on his chest and call out to him with no answer. Ron entered the room and stood there in disbelief. Daddy was gone. The nursing staff worked tirelessly on him to revive him and placed him on life support. The doctor explained his heart had completely given out, and there was nothing more they could do. We had to make a decision to unplug the machines.

I remember the feeling of completeness, as I began to pray for direction. God had him now. Daddy had given his life back to the Lord on his deathbed. He was now in the presence of Jesus. "My plans will be revealed in you." I remembered those nights back in October and November when the Holy Spirit spoke directly to me and told me not to fear or be afraid. I was comforted in knowing God's will had been done. My Daddy made it to heaven. Amazing! What love the Lord has for each one of us, even for those who don't deserve His love. I am satisfied in knowing I was used through the trials to grow and learn to forgive before it was too late.

I thank God I obeyed the call to carry the burdens brought into my father's life. My flesh wanted to leave him a prison cell because of the past and present troubles. He didn't deserve my love, compassion, sacrifice, and forgiveness. I didn't deserve to have a Savior lay down His life for ME so that I could have everlasting life. I completely forgave, and I'm forgiven.

CHAPTER 40

HEALING BEGINS

I MEANT I WOULD HONOR a man who gave his heart and life to the Lord. It mattered not whether he abused and abandoned his wife and children years earlier. I would not have anyone speaking at his funeral that would remotely mention his alcoholism and abuse. Instead, I found those old friends who knew his work ethic and his supernatural strength. I found old childhood friends that visited him on his deathbed and prayed with him before he passed. I was going to honor thy father in spite of all of the turmoil. He was forgiven, and it really didn't matter if I had forgiven him or not. He had been forgiven by the King of Kings and Lord of Lords. Oh, but I had. I had been released by the bonds of unforgiveness, hatred, and resentment. I was free! I could start the journey of picking up the pieces of my life.

After the funeral, I received condolences through cards, letters, and phone calls. I also received some from the funeral home website. One message called out to me more than any other one. It was my oldest sister, Dana's mother, Judy. Mrs. Judy sent the sweetest message to our family. I was ecstatic. I didn't want to bombard her with replies so soon after she had written, but I just had to write her back. I wanted to meet my sister, Dana! I had wanted to meet her all of my life.

It had been six months since Daddy had passed, and I had never had the chance to speak with Mrs. Judy about my sister. I told myself to take it slow, and if it were meant to be, it would happen. Mrs. Judy and I formed a friendship via email, and one day she offered to let me and Carol meet Dana for the first time.

We planned our meeting at a local country club restaurant for lunch that day. It was February 10th. Carol and I happily jumped in the car and drove to meet our big sister. Nervous and filled with anxiety, we sat in the car waiting for her to arrive. As Dana came zooming up on her car, I told Carol I'd bet that was her by the way that she drove. The most beautiful lady bounced out of the car, and when our eyes met across the parking lot, we instantly knew we were sisters. The feeling of nervousness left, as we embraced for the very first time as siblings. We would never be separated again by life's circumstances.

Our lunch turned into dinner as we shared from our hearts with one another tears, laughter, and sincerity—bonded for life. God had given me the greatest gift through all of the pain. Dana was the sweetest, most giving and compassionate person. I was so thankful to call her my sister. I was so thankful to God for giving me this gift at this particular time in my life; truly an added blessing for my obedience to His perfect plan of forgiveness unforgettable.

<u>Interesting detail</u>:

The final edited version of this story was completed on the four
year anniversary of my Daddy's death.

~Forgiveness Unforgettable~

Made in the USA
Columbia, SC
25 April 2019